FULVIA

WOMEN IN ANTIQUITY

Series Editors: Ronnie Ancona and Sarah B. Pomeroy

This book series provides compact and accessible introductions to the life and historical times of women from the ancient world. Approaching ancient history and culture broadly, the series selects figures from the earliest of times to late antiquity.

Cleopatra
A Biography
Duane W. Roller

Clodia Metelli
The Tribune's Sister
Marilyn B. Skinner

Galla Placidia
The Last Roman Empress
Hagith Sivan

Arsinoë of Egypt and Macedon
A Royal Life
Elizabeth Donnelly Carney

Berenice II and the Golden Age of Ptolemaic Egypt
Dee L. Clayman

Faustina I and II
Imperial Women of the Golden Age
Barbara M. Levick

Turia
A Roman Woman's Civil War
Josiah Osgood

Monica
An Ordinary Saint
Gillian Clark

Theodora
Actress, Empress, Saint
David Potter

Hypatia
The Life and Legend of an Ancient Philosopher
Edward Watts

Boudica
Warrior Woman of Roman Britain
Caitlin C. Gillespie

Sabina Augusta
An Imperial Journey
T. Corey Brennan

Cleopatra's Daughter
And Other Royal Woman of the Augustan Era
Duane W. Roller

Perpetua
Athlete of God
Barbara K. Gold

Zenobia
Shooting Star of Palmyra
Nathanael Andrade

Eurydice and the Birth of Macedonian Power
Elizabeth Donnelly Carney

Melania the Younger
From Rome to Jerusalem
Elizabeth A. Clark

Sosipatra of Pergamum
Philosopher and Oracle
Heidi Marx

FULVIA

PLAYING FOR POWER AT THE END OF THE ROMAN REPUBLIC

Celia E. Schultz

Oxford University Press is a department of the University of Oxford. It furthers
the University's objective of excellence in research, scholarship, and education
by publishing worldwide. Oxford is a registered trade mark of Oxford University
Press in the UK and certain other countries.

Published in the United States of America by Oxford University Press
198 Madison Avenue, New York, NY 10016, United States of America.

© Oxford University Press 2021

All rights reserved. No part of this publication may be reproduced, stored in
a retrieval system, or transmitted, in any form or by any means, without the
prior permission in writing of Oxford University Press, or as expressly permitted
by law, by license, or under terms agreed with the appropriate reproduction
rights organization. Inquiries concerning reproduction outside the scope of the
above should be sent to the Rights Department, Oxford University Press, at the
address above.

You must not circulate this work in any other form
and you must impose this same condition on any acquirer.

Library of Congress Cataloging-in-Publication Data
Names: Schultz, Celia E., author.
Title: Fulvia : playing for power at the end of the Roman republic / Celia E. Schultz.
Other titles: Women in antiquity.
Description: New York : Oxford University Press, [2021] |
Series: Women in antiquity | Includes bibliographical references and index.
Identifiers: LCCN 2021007932 (print) | LCCN 2021007933 (ebook) |
ISBN 9780197601839 (paperback) | ISBN 9780190697136 (hardback) |
ISBN 9780190697150 (epub) | ISBN 9780190697143 (updf) |
ISBN 9780190697167 (oso)
Subjects: LCSH: Fulvia, active 1st century B.C. | Women—Rome—Biography. |
Rome—History—Republic, 265–30 B.C.
Classification: LCC DG260.F85 S34 2021 (print) |
LCC DG260.F85 (ebook) | DDC 937/.05092 [B]—dc23
LC record available at https://lccn.loc.gov/2021007932
LC ebook record available at https://lccn.loc.gov/2021007933

DOI: 10.1093/oso/9780190697136.001.0001

For my mother,
Susann Esther Feingold-Schultz,
who would have enjoyed this project

Contents

List of Illustrations ix
Acknowledgments xi
Abbreviations xiii
Maps xiv

1. The Background   1
2. Fulvia Enters the Scene   19
3. Life with Curio and Antonius   49
4. Fulvia's Final Act   73
5. After Fulvia's Death   104

Bibliography   119
Index   127

Illustrations

Maps

Map of the Roman Empire in 44 BCE.   xiv
Map of Rome in the Late Republic.   xvi

Figures

1.1. Fulvia's family tree.   9
1.2. A coin bearing Fulvia's portrait (?).   14
2.1. The *gens Claudia*.   21
2.2. Altar set up by Claudia Syntyche, Museo Capitolino, Rome.   24
2.3. Denarius of C. Clodius Vestalis.   25
3.1. Bust of Antonius, Museo Arqueológico Nacional, Madrid.   62
3.2. The *gens Antonia*.   64
4.1. Sling bullet with an insult for Fulvia.   97
5.1. The Royal Mausoleum of Mauretania in Algeria.   109
5.2. Funeral vase of Claudius, son of Fulvia and Clodius.   112
5.3. P. A. Svedomsky, *Fulvia with the Head of Cicero*.   114

Acknowledgments

I am very grateful to Sarah Pomeroy and Ronnie Ancona, the editors of Oxford University Press's *Women in Antiquity* series, for the invitation to add a volume on Fulvia, whom I have long considered the most interesting of a whole cohort of remarkable aristocratic women who took part in the major events of the last decades of Rome's Republic. It is high time that Fulvia take her place on the bookshelf alongside her more famous contemporaries who have already received biographies of their own in this series and outside it: her sister-in-law, Clodia; her romantic successor, Cleopatra, Queen of Egypt; Terentia and Tullia, the wife and daughter of Fulvia's *bête noire*, Cicero; and Servilia, the mother of an enemy of one of her husbands. Even the unnamed woman commonly known as "Turia" already has a volume to herself.

In keeping with the mission of this series, I have aimed to make Fulvia as accessible to as many readers as possible, while at the same time providing enough references in the notes to make this book useful to those who might want to pursue their own research. I have therefore limited citations, for the most part, to recent and important Anglophone scholarship, and I have eschewed comprehensive lists of ancient references. For tales of Fulvia and her contemporaries, I have usually cited only the fullest or most famous versions found in ancient authors.

This book is, as any book is, the product of a lot of assistance from many people. Lorena Bolaños Abarca helped with translations of Spanish-language publications. Lucio Benedetti tracked down other, more elusive publications and generously shared the image of the sling bullet that appears in Chapter 4. Nathan Elkins, Olya Weber, and Molly Swetnam-Burland helped track down images. Kelly Hardy navigated a week-long road trip through central and northern Italy to see collections of sling bullets. Mafalda Cipollone and Luana Cenciaioli provided access to the collection in the Museo Archeologico Nazionale dell'Umbria in Perugia; Carolina Ascari Raccagni gave us a tour of the Museo Archeologico Statale di Ascoli Piceno and a lovely introduction to the town. Once I returned home, Alan Taub, at the University of Michigan School of Engineering, and his students helpfully consulted on the properties of lead. Jessica Clark, Elizabeth Greene, Gwynaeth McIntyre, Patrick Tansey, Tom Hillard, Josiah Osgood, and Kathryn Welch all patiently answered numerous questions. Kathryn Welch and Judith Hallett also graciously shared some of their unpublished research. Stefan Vranka and his staff at OUP kept me on track, and an anonymous reviewer offered many sharp-eyed suggestions for improvement. John Muccigrosso, Glenn Storey, Stephen Wheeler, Lynn Orr, Davida Manon, Miriam Manon, and especially Kathryn Welch all read early drafts of parts of this project. Audiences at the Pennsylvania State University, the University of Mississippi, and the University of Colorado let me test out some ideas, as did my students and colleagues at the University of Michigan. Julia Jeffs created the three stemmata included here, and Jan Dewitt weeded out numerous errors and omissions in the typescript. I put the finishing touches on this project during a delightful year at the Swedish Collegium for Advanced Study. Whatever erroneous bits remain are my own responsibility. I owe special thanks to Fulvia, for having such an interesting life that falls neatly into five chapters, complete with climax and dénouement.

Finally, this book is dedicated to my mother, who taught me how to write and who edited everything I published until six years ago, when Alzheimer's disease began to fog the clarity of her thought. I hope that she knows, at some deep level, how much I am grateful for everything.

Celia Schultz
Ann Arbor
May 2021

Abbreviations

All abbreviations for Greek and Roman writers and their works follow the format found in the Oxford Classical Dictionary (https://oxfordre.com/classics/page/abbreviation-list/).

BNP	H. Cancik and H. Schneider, eds., *Brill's New Pauly: Encyclopaedia of the Ancient World, Antiquity*. 16 vols. Leiden: Brill, 2002–2010.
CIL	*Corpus Inscriptionum Latinarum*. Berlin: de Gruyter, 1893–.
FRHist	T. J. Cornell, ed., *The Fragments of the Roman Historians*. 3 vols. Oxford: Oxford University Press, 2013.
ILS	H. Dessau, *Inscriptiones Latinae Selectae*. 3 vols. Berlin: Weidmann, 1892–1916.
Inscr. Ital.	A. Degrassi, *Inscriptiones Italiae*. 13 vols. Rome: Libreria dello Stato, 1931–1986.
MRR	T. R. S. Broughton, *Magistrates of the Roman Republic*, 3 vols. New York: American Philological Association, 1951–1960.
RRC	M. H. Crawford, *Roman Republican Coinage*, 2 vols. New York: American Philologocal Association, 1974.
SBA	D. R. Shackleton Bailey, *Cicero's Letters to Atticus*, 7 vols. Cambridge: Cambridge University Press, 1965–1971.
SBF	D. R. Shackleton Bailey, *Cicero: Epistulae ad Familiares*, 2 vols. Cambridge: Cambridge University Press, 1977.

Map of the Roman Empire in 44 BCE.

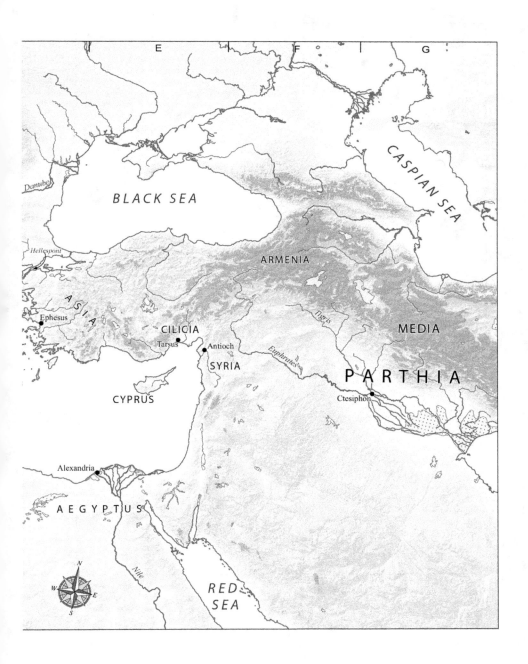

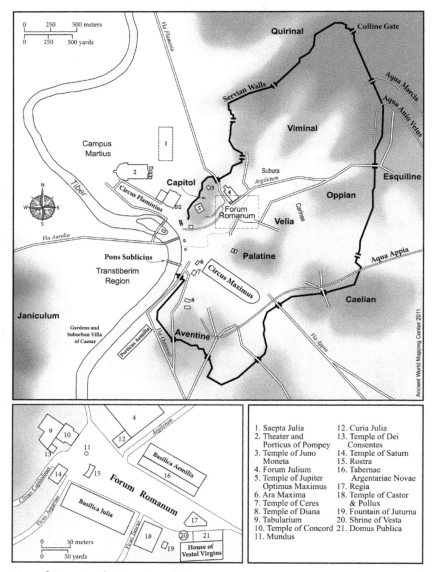

Map of Rome in the Late Republic.

1

The Background

Fulvia, daughter of Marcus Fulvius Bambalio and Sempronia, is one of the most flamboyant and most reviled figures from the last decades of the Roman Republic. She was for a time—the years 44 to 41 BCE, when her husband, Antonius, was the most powerful man in the city—the most prominent woman in Rome. Over the course of her life, she is said to have masterminded a riot in the Roman Forum that resulted in the burning of the senate house, dominated her husbands, meddled in politics, and started a war with the future emperor Augustus. Cicero, the great orator and stateman, calls her "the most avaricious of women," and the biographer Plutarch says that Fulvia preferred to rule a ruler and command a commander.[1]

In Fulvia's day, the proper domain for an aristocratic Roman woman was her household, which she should run efficiently, graciously, and demurely. Even so, women of Fulvia's class were not hidden away in their homes. Theater, games, festivals, and social visits drew them out. Nor, when at home, were they relegated strictly to domestic duties. It is quite clear from our sources—the very same sources that advertise the feminine domestic ideal—that aristocratic women also took on active roles in their families' affairs, including financial matters and the political careers of their brothers, husbands, and sons. They could control a visitor's or a client's access to the powerful men in the household, and they offered valued counsel in discussions of policy and strategy. But it was expected that this would be done discreetly, behind closed doors. A woman should not draw the public's attention to herself, nor should

---

1. Cic., *Phil.* 6.4; Plut., *Ant.* 10.3.

she preempt male prerogative.² Fulvia's fault was that she was too visible, too public.

The ancient sources give us a Fulvia who is brash, rude, domineering, ambitious not just for her husbands but for herself, and petty—a caricature of a powerful, independent woman. She has suffered almost as badly among some modern writers, who often depict her as the antithesis of matronal virtue, a truly wicked woman, "ambitious, jealous, cruel, avaricious, and vengeful, she made herself mistress of Rome and ruled Italy with a capricious tyranny, which surpassed even that of the triumvirs."³ Others, more sympathetic, emphasize her political skill and her loyalty to her husbands, especially Antonius, but they still leave largely unchallenged the ancient stories of her cruelty and greed.⁴ In husbands—of whom Antonius was the last—she preferred men cut from the same cloth as she: disreputable, even treacherous men who were willing to undermine Rome's republican government in order to advance themselves.

We feel like we know Fulvia. But even though you hold her biography in your hands, we know relatively little about her for certain. Our sources preserve nothing of her life before her first marriage and very little about her life after it. We do not know how she spent most of her days, who were her friends, whom she found tedious, what she enjoyed reading, what she thought of her life and her husbands and children, how she wanted to be perceived, what drove her to act in such bold and public ways. We do not have any of her own writings, if she ever produced any. Nor do we have an ancient account of her that achieves anything like an objective assessment. What we do have, however, is an impressive array of contemporary, thoroughly hostile accounts, written by men whose main interest was to target Fulvia's husbands. As is often the case with ancient women, we only know something about Fulvia because she was caught up in the political wranglings of men in high office.⁵ Indeed, the Fulvia who comes down to us is, in large part, the product of the imaginations of her husbands' enemies.

---

2. Although it describes circumstances outside Rome under the empire, Hemelrijk's formulation of the public role of women applies to the city in Fulvia's day (Hemelrijk 2015, 10–12).

3. Abbott 1909, 72. Balsdon (1962, 49) describes her as an "Amazon of a woman . . . an infinitely loyal virago." De la Bédoyère accepts uncritically ancient claims that Fulvia "presided over politics in Rome, enjoying unprecedented power and influence for a woman" (2018, 47).

4. See, for example, Bauman 1992, 83–90, and Virlouvet 2001.

5. On the construction of matronal norms in late Republican literature and the reaction to women (esp. Fulvia) who transgress them, see Brennan 2012 and Hallett 2015.

Of the writers who pay Fulvia any attention, by far the most important for recovering what we can about her is Marcus Tullius Cicero, a powerful politician and orator who raised defamation to an art form and who was happy to bend the truth to persuade and entertain his audience. By the time Fulvia enters the historical record, in her mid-twenties, Cicero was already in his mid-fifties, more than a decade past the height of his political career (his consulship of 63 BCE). He had long been a political opponent of her first and third husbands, Clodius and Antonius, and it is through his written attacks against them that many stories about Fulvia are preserved.

The other important contemporary source for the information that we have about Fulvia is Octavian, the young man who would eventually become Rome's first emperor, Augustus. But truth be told, we have almost nothing of what he himself wrote about her, beyond a scrap of scandalous poetry. Of greater significance than the poem, however, would be his autobiography, if it were not lost to the ages. Fortunately, it influenced later accounts of the events of the day, including those that are still available to us, so we can glean from them what Octavian may have said. It is safe to say that Octavian was not a fan.

Octavian came from a senatorial family, but he only came to real prominence at the age of nineteen, when he inherited the name and the estate of his great uncle, Gaius Julius Caesar, who was dictator at Rome at the time of his death. Caesar never had a legitimate son of his own, and his only grandchild died a few days after being born,[6] so in his will, Caesar proclaimed his sister's grandson as his primary heir.[7] Later,

---

6. The only child Caesar recognized as his own was a daughter, Julia, who died in 53 after giving birth to her child by Pompey. The child died shortly thereafter (Plut., *Vit. Caes.* 23.5–7; Suet., *Iul.* 26.1). Caesar appears to have had a son by Cleopatra, the queen of Egypt. She claimed that the boy, born in 47 BCE after Caesar's extended sojourn in Alexandria, was Caesar's. The fact that Caesar allowed the boy to be called Ptolemy Caesar (he is better known now by his popular nickname, Caesarion, "Little Caesar") strongly suggests that Caesar believed this to be true, but it is not clear that he ever formally acknowledged paternity. Some years later, in an effort to derail the activities of Octavian, Caesar's heir, Antonius, claimed that Caesar had, in fact, officially accepted Caesarion as his own. Octavian's allies disputed the claim. See Suet., *Iul.* 52.1–2. Despite Octavian's challenge to Caesarion's claim, he was still sufficiently threatened by the boy's potential as a political rival that he executed him immediately after the end of his war with Antonius (the story is told at Plut., *Vit. Ant.* 81.2–82.1). A good summary of what we know of Caesarion can be found in Gray-Fow 2014.

7. Octavian worked hard to ensure that people thought of him not only as Caesar's heir but as Caesar's son, even going so far as to insist on the passage of a *lex curiata*, a law that conferred upon him the legal status of Caesar's son, in the late summer or early autumn of 43, a year and a half after Caesar's death. Consensus among scholars is that Caesar's will did not, indeed could not, legally move Octavian from his own clan, the *gens Octavia*, into Caesar's family. Such a transfer is the goal of a proper adoption (Latin, *adoptio*), but it was not possible at Rome through a will. This process, referred to in English as testamentary adoption, is a concept that was not known to ancient jurists.

as the emperor Augustus, Octavian controlled the developing historical narrative about the last decades of the Republic, in ways both direct and indirect—an excellent instance of the truism that victors, or at least authors of whom they approve, write the history books. Texts written three hundred years after Fulvia's death preserve aspects of the blisteringly hostile portrayal of her that Augustus promoted.

This book takes a fresh look at Fulvia by identifying and disengaging the biases in our sources, all the while being careful not to cross too far into the territory of undue rehabilitation. Let us be clear: to some extent, her reputation for brashness and aggression is well deserved. The work presented here, however, aims to recover, to the extent possible, what we can know about the real, historical Fulvia. This project requires taking into account the full sweep of the available evidence, rather than privileging some of the more scandalous stories we have about her—like the time she calculatingly displayed her grief, along with her dead husband's broken body, to the mob gathered outside her house in order to spark a riot, or the time that she vented her anger by stabbing the tongue of Cicero's severed head with a hairpin—and ignoring other, less flashy scraps of information. Such tantalizing tales capture the imagination, but are unlikely to get us, in any straightforward way, to Fulvia herself. The stories about Fulvia also need to be set within the context of what other aristocratic Roman women were doing in the last decades of the Republic—and what was said about them.

The Fulvia who emerges in the pages that follow was a strong-willed, independent woman of sufficient propriety that, at two different points in her life, people saw her as a potential mate who could provide ballast and respectability to a politician whose career was careening out of control. She was more daring and more visible than any of her contemporaries except Cleopatra: this was what made her a target of politically motivated mudslinging. Fulvia was clearly attractive in her own right: she was never single for long, and her marriages seem to have been successful by Roman standards: they produced children (especially sons) and they lasted until one partner died. She seems to have been

---

What Caesar offered his great-nephew in his will was three-fourths of his estate on the condition that the young man take on his name (*condicio nominis ferendi*). A clear and concise summary of the issues—and discussion of the late republican cases—is found in Konrad 1996, 124–7 (especially p. 125 n. 107) with Linderski 1996, 152–4, in the same volume. The extended discussion of Octavian's adoption in Lindsay 2009 (182–9 with 79–86 on testamentary adoption generally) arrives at the same conclusion, but his analysis is less crystalline.

a chaste wife: except for one passing comment by Cicero and a ribald poem by Octavian, there was never even a hint of sexual impropriety on her part in the historical sources. Finally, like many elite Roman women of her day, Fulvia proved that she had political acumen on par with (and occasionally surpassing that of) the men around her. On numerous occasions she championed her husbands' interests—especially at times when they were not in a position to do so themselves. It was not at all unusual for the women of Rome's great political families to actively assist and advise their husbands, sons, and brothers on matters of public importance. It is clear that as the Republic was falling apart, aristocratic women did not sit idly by, tending only to dinner party menus and fixing their hair. Like the men with whom they lived, for these women politics was of supreme importance. What makes Fulvia stand out among her peers, however, is that her role in events of the Republic's last decades was sometimes center stage, whereas most of her contemporaries were content to work behind the scenes.

Political Background

Before detailing what can be known about Fulvia, however, it will be helpful to sketch the world in which she lived. The year of her birth has to be estimated backward from the date of her first marriage, around 60 BCE, to Publius Clodius Pulcher. Following Roman custom for upper-class young women, Fulvia was probably in her mid-teens at the time of her wedding, putting her birth somewhere in the early to mid-70s.[8] Her death occurred in 40 BCE, when Fulvia was in her mid-to late 30s. Thus her life spanned a very difficult, chaotic period of Roman history. She will have witnessed her city invaded by its own troops several times, the assassination of prominent politicians (including her first husband), food shortages, pirate scares, and riots and gang violence in the streets.

The danger and chaos in Rome of the 50s and 40s were nothing new: by then, the Republic had been ripping itself apart for several generations. Shortly before Fulvia's arrival in the world, Rome emerged from Sulla's brutal dictatorship when he voluntarily retired from his position in 79 and died shortly thereafter. The dictatorship was itself the culmination of the first few rounds of Roman civil war that had been

---

8. Fischer puts her birth in 75 (1999, 8).

brought about by the increased fracturing of Roman society. Fault lines developed between groups that had, in earlier ages, pursued largely the same interests: senators and equestrians, who were just as wealthy (if not wealthier) than their senatorial counterparts but who had chosen to pursue business over politics; Roman elites and aristocrats from towns elsewhere in Italy; the urban poor and the soldiery. More rounds of civil war would follow after Sulla, with the last, between Octavian and Antonius, happening after Fulvia's death. Ultimately, Rome's republican form of government—where the core of power and control was the collective body of the Roman senate—weakened almost to the point of disintegration. In its place would arise an inherited monarchy with Augustus as its first emperor.

Political power was the *raison d'être* for Rome's most important clans (Latin *gentes*, sing. *gens*), including Fulvia's family and the families of each of her husbands. Roman aristocrats, whether from one of the truly ancient families called patrician or the (relatively) more recently ennobled plebeian clans, did everything within their power to further their own political careers and those of their friends and relatives. Women, of course, could not hold political office, but families and clans understood that daughters, sisters, and wives could be very useful pawns in the political game. In some cases, they could also be valuable advisors, go-betweens, and power brokers. Political alliances were sometimes reinforced by marriage arrangements, and a family whose sons had not achieved the most desirable offices (especially the truly powerful positions of praetor and consul, which sat at the top of Rome's political ladder) could improve its fortunes by marrying a daughter to someone with more exciting prospects.

The political landscape at Rome in the last decades of the Republic (roughly from 133 BCE until the end in 31 BCE) was a rough-and-tumble place. Competition for public office was fierce, and alliances shifted frequently, often with dizzying speed. In the pages that follow, some effort has been made to streamline, but not distort, this aspect of our story. Bribery of voters and jurors was increasingly common, and some politicians (including Fulvia's first husband, Clodius) were not above using armed gangs to suppress their political opponents. Political careers were rarely ideologically driven in the way we are accustomed to see now. Roman politicians in this period did not generally attach themselves to a cause or an agenda in the way a modern politician can spend decades fighting against government regulation or advocating for the rights of the poor, although there were some exceptions to this rule. For the most part, men acted in what they saw as the Republic's—and their own—best interest at the moment. Rome had nothing like today's political parties with their consistent, recognizable platforms. Alliances were constantly being formed, dissolved, and then reconstituted.

Perhaps the most important political division during Fulvia's lifetime had more to do with the source of a politician's power rather than adherence to a particular position on a given issue. Optimates were conservatives who prized the traditional authority of the senate, whereas populists (the English derives from the Latin, *popularis*) drew their power from their popularity with voters. A man might shift from populist to optimate and back again as it suited his purposes, even if his personal position on a given issue did not change at all. Familial links are not necessarily good predictors of a man's political alignment. Among Fulvia's husbands, the full gamut is represented. Clodius came from a patrician clan, one of Rome's oldest, most prestigious families, yet he made his career as a populist who advanced legislation to help the urban poor in order to ensure that they propelled him further up the political ladder in future elections. Curio, Fulvia's second husband, and Antonius were also aristocrats, but from plebeian clans. Whereas Clodius's family had been involved in politics at the highest level almost since the founding of the Republic in 509 BCE, the Curiones and the Antonii were relatively new arrivals to the pinnacle of power. Curio was, for almost his entire career, an optimate, but he rather dramatically aligned himself with the populist Caesar at a critical moment in 49 BCE. It is difficult to pin a label on Antonius, but he was famously loyal to Caesar, his long-time commanding officer. Caesar was himself a patrician populist. About Fulvia's political opinions, one can only speculate.[9]

Integrally related to the optimate–populist divide was another of the defining tensions in Roman society in the first century BCE: the increasing struggle for dominance between the senate and a long series of individual politicians, especially those who stood at the head of an army. In the Roman Republic, military and political leaders were drawn from

---

9. In Appian's account of the war at Perusia, discussed in Chapter 4, the figure of Antonius's brother, Lucius, distinguishes his own republican leanings from Fulvia's commitment to monarchy (*B. Civ.* 5.54). There are good reasons not to accept Lucius's assertion (see pp. 94–95), which may mean nothing more than that she remained steadfastly supportive of Antonius. One should certainly not take the passing reference as a strong indication that Fulvia was a "true Caesarian" (Bauman 1992, 89).

The Background

the same pool. At about the time of Fulvia's marriage to Clodius, Rome saw an unprecedented type of coordinated opposition to senatorial control in the formation of a political alliance among a triad of powerful individuals: the most important general of the day, Gnaeus Pompeius Magnus (Pompey the Great); one of Rome's wealthiest men who also had a well-established political career, Marcus Licinius Crassus; and Gaius Julius Caesar, a rising political star. They are sometimes called, incorrectly, the First Triumvirate;[10] some historians now prefer to call them the Three. Whatever moniker one chooses for them, these men were united in their opposition to the Roman senate. The senate's conservative optimate faction had prevented Pompey from obtaining land for his veterans and failed to grant him the final ratification of his recent restructuring of Rome's eastern territories. Crassus was at odds with much the same group over a reduction in the price of the tax-farming contract for the province of Asia, which would have been a huge boon to his allies among the equestrian class who owned the companies that brought in tax revenue from around the empire. For his part, Caesar wanted the consulship, the most powerful magistracy in Rome, but he needed money for his campaign and voters who would be reliable—two things Pompey and Crassus could provide. Their partnership, tenuous from its foundation and acrimonious in its dissolution, set in motion the series of events that shaped many of the major events in Fulvia's adult life.

Family Background

Fulvia was the only child of Marcus Fulvius Bambalio and his wife, Sempronia. Her father's clan, the *gens Fulvia* (Figure 1.1), was one of

---

10. Technically, the term "triumvirate" should refer to an officially appointed or elected board of three men (*tresviri, triumviri*) endowed with specific legal powers. Such boards were common in the Republic, for example, *tresviri monetales* (Board of Three Men for Minting Coins) and *tresviri coloniae deductae* (for Settling the Colony). The "First Triumvirate" never had any official standing; it always remained an informal alliance among Pompey, Crassus, and Caesar. Ancient writers call it a *societas* ("partnership") or a *conspiratio* ("union" or, more negatively, "conspiracy"). The misleading moniker is a relatively modern invention, inspired by the later, legitimate triumvirate of Octavian, Antonius, and Lepidus, who were granted extraordinary powers and the title of *triumviri rei publicae constituendae* (for the Consolidation of the State) by law in 43 BCE. The earliest use of "triumvirate" to describe the alliance of Pompey, Crassus, and Caesar appears in the late sixteenth century, but widespread use does not develop until the mid-eighteenth century. See Ridley 1999 and Sanders 1932.

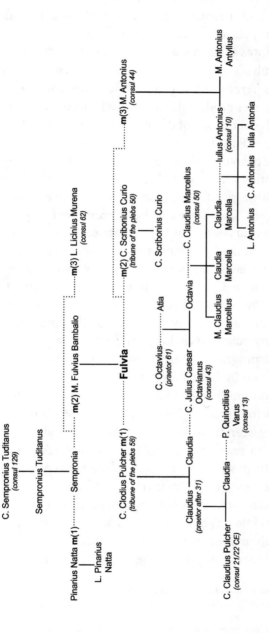

FIGURE 1.1. Fulvia's family tree (J. Jeffs).

several prominent Roman families originally from Tusculum (modern Frascati), an old Latin town that lay fifteen miles southeast of Rome. Tusculum's residents received Roman citizenship early on (381 BCE) yet retained their autonomy, and Tusculan aristocrats, including Fulvia's family, had been active in politics at Rome for centuries by the time Fulvia was born. The town was a fashionable spot for the country homes of Rome's elite. Among Fulvia's contemporaries who maintained villas there were Cicero; Marcus Terentius Varro, a prolific writer and one of the greatest scholars Rome ever produced; and Lucius Licinius Lucullus, a successful politician and general, one of Rome's wealthiest men, and at one point, husband of one of Fulvia's sisters-in-law.[11]

Fulvia appears to have been one of the last, if not the last, surviving members of both her mother's and her father's families, a status that seems to have left her with a substantial financial inheritance.[12] Both the *gens Fulvia* and the *gens Sempronia* had been prominent in politics through the second century BCE, but both disappear from the list of consuls in the aftermath of the Gracchan crisis, a pivotal moment in Roman history that is bracketed by the political careers of two brothers, Tiberius and Gaius Sempronius Gracchus, both of whom held the political office of tribune of the plebs, in 133 and 123–1, respectively. The Gracchi were powerful populist politicians who drew on the strength of their loyal following among voters to challenge the senate's supremacy and to advance legislative programs designed to benefit Rome's poor. Their opponents—threatened by what they saw as an attempt to curb their own power and to diminish their livelihood—responded with a level of brutality never before seen in Roman politics: both brothers died violently in melees between their supporters and their rivals.

The last Sempronius to reach the consulship was Fulvia's great-grandfather in 129 BCE. His position with regard to the Gracchi is unclear. The last Fulvius to serve as consul (in 125) was a close ally of Gaius Gracchus. Fulvius and his two sons died fighting alongside him in 121.[13] Extrapolating from what is known about the consul of 125, it sometimes asserted that Fulvia's family maintained its populist leanings over several generations,[14] but this cannot be proved one way or the other.

11. For the sources on the Tusculan villas of the Rome's rich and famous, see McCracken 1942. Fulvia's Tusculan origins: Cic., *Phil.* 3.16. Tusculum and Roman citizenship: Liv. 6.25.6–6.26.8; Cic., *Planc.* 8.19.
12. Most of the money seems to have come from her mother's family (Fischer 1999, 11–12).
13. Syme 2016, 173–85.
14. For example, Virlouvet 2001, 67.

It is not clear exactly how Fulvia's father was related to more prominent members of his clan, including the consul of 125. Bambalio's name has the proper form for a Roman aristocratic man: his individual name, Marcus, followed by his clan name, Fulvius, and a nickname (called a *cognomen* in Latin). The only item missing from the records is his patronymic: in legal contexts, Romans identified themselves as "son of...." Because the *gens Fulvia* was a large family, many of its members used a cognomen to identify the branch to which they belonged. Sometimes these were complimentary, such as Nobilior ("rather noble"), but others were less flattering, such as Flaccus ("with ears that stick out"). Yet even these were borne proudly by Roman aristocrats. Numerous Fulvii Nobiliores and Fulvii Flacci held high political office in earlier times. In other cases, individuals bore nicknames unique to themselves. One such individual is Fulvia's father, whose cognomen, Bambalio, is derived from the Greek verb meaning "to stammer." Cicero confirmed that the man had a speech impediment when he dismissed him as "a man of no account, than whom nothing is more contemptible because he bears an insulting nickname due to his hesitating speech and his stupidity."[15] Bambalio's stammer would explain his failure to launch a successful political career, for which excellence in public speaking was essential. There is no evidence that Fulvia's father ever ran for, let alone held, public office.

Fulvia and her mother, Sempronia, like all Roman women of their day, officially bore only a single name, the feminine form of their fathers' clan name: Fulvia was so named because her father was a Fulvius. Sisters would technically have the same formal name, but would distinguish among themselves with nicknames, which were sometimes as impersonal as *Maior / Minor* (the Elder / the Younger) or a numerical designation like *Prima, Secunda, Tertia* (the First, Second, Third). Like their male relatives, women, too, further identified themselves with a patronymic. Scholars sometimes refer to Fulvia as Fulvia Flacca Bambula, but this is a modern creation based on assumptions about her father's relationship to other, more famous Fulvii. The only name that we know her by from ancient sources is Fulvia.[16]

Sempronia's family was rather distinguished. Her grandfather, Gaius Sempronius Tuditanus, was the last Sempronius to hold the consulship.

---

15. Cic., *Phil.* 3.16.
16. Keegan 2020, 103.

Tuditanus's son, Sempronia's father, however, must have been a disappointment. He held no political office, so far as we know, and he had a reputation for eccentricity, dressing like a stage actor (a lower-class occupation, inappropriate for the son of a consul), and is reported to have gotten up on the speaker's platform in the Roman Forum and scattered money to the crowd below. Some said he was mad and hallucinated. Despite his unseemly generosity, he had plenty of money to leave Sempronia, his only child, in his will. The estate was large enough to be worth fighting over: a relative challenged Sempronius's will in court. The man lost the case, and Sempronia was able to take up her inheritance.[17]

Sempronia married three times.[18] Her first husband was an otherwise unknown Lucius (?) Pinarius Natta, with whom she had a son who would one day serve as a *pontifex*, one of the most important priesthoods in Rome. It is not clear if Sempronia was divorced or widowed when she took up with her second husband, Bambalio, nor is it clear how her second marriage ended.[19] Although both of her first two husbands hailed from wealthy, aristocratic families, it was with her third husband, L. Licinius Murena, that Sempronia—and her children—achieved the highest level of social prominence.[20] Murena, whose family had only gotten as far as the praetorship in earlier generations, was himself elected consul for 62 BCE. His victory at the polls was marred by a charge of having bribed voters, but his defense team (including Crassus and Cicero) successfully argued for his acquittal. His consulship was relatively uneventful.

There has long been a question about whether Fulvia's mother is the same Sempronia named by the historian Sallust as a member of a conspiracy headed by Lucius Sergius Catilina, better known in English as Catiline.[21] There is also a Fulvia in Sallust's account, but this woman—old enough to be the mistress of one of the conspirators—cannot possibly be

---

17. The court case: Val. Max. 7.8.1. On Sempronia's father's eccentricities, see Cic., *Acad.* 2.89 and *Phil.* 3.16.

18. The evidence for Sempronia's marital history is complicated and the sources are only partial. I follow L. R. Taylor's reconstruction (Taylor 1942: 396–7, n. 34), which has since found widespread acceptance among historians.

19. That Sempronia and Bambalio divorced is perhaps implied by a passing reference at Cass. Dio 45.47.4 to a friendly relationship between Antonius and Fulvia's father, suggesting that Bambalio survived at least until his daughter's third marriage. But the reference, if based in reality, may well refer to a time long before Antonius took up with Fulvia.

20. Sempronia's marriage to Murena may have produced another half-brother for Fulvia, A. Terentius Varro Murena. See Babcock 1965, 6–7 n. 14.

21. For a selective summary of opinions, see Delia 1991, 209 n. 11.

our Fulvia, who was likely not yet even a teenager when the conspirators attempted to bring down the Roman government in 63, the year that Cicero and Antonius's uncle, Gaius Antonius Hybrida, were consuls.

Sallust's Sempronia is the very embodiment of the decadence of Catiline and his followers, a group of aristocrats who owed too much money and craved more power than they had been able to obtain through legal means. This Sempronia was noble and beautiful; educated, refined, and witty—although Sallust censoriously reports that she danced and sang with more skill than a proper lady should. She was also blessed with a good husband and children. Sallust's Sempronia was profligate with her money and reputation and, perhaps most scandalous of all, she was capable of deeds only a man should be brave enough to do (*virilis audaciae facinora*)—including lying and being an accessory to murder.[22]

Such a woman would indeed be a fitting mother for our Fulvia, who was herself a woman so involved in politics and war that she was described by the Roman historian Velleius Paterculus as having nothing feminine about her but for her physical form.[23] Unfortunately, there is no ancient evidence for a connection: no ancient author—most importantly, Cicero, who was the consul who suppressed the conspiracy and who, in later years, delivered some blistering public attacks on Fulvia—ever links her to the Catilinarian Sempronia. Sir Ronald Syme, perhaps the most important Roman historian of the twentieth century, subscribed to the theory that Catiline's Sempronia was Fulvia's aunt,[24] her mother's sister, but it is impossible to know. Given that every woman born into a clan was identified by a feminine form of the clan name, it is probable that there were more than a few Sempronias in Rome in the late 60s BCE.

Fulvia Herself

Much of what we know about Fulvia pertains to her adult life, but even so, there is much about her that remains a mystery. Among the things we do not know is what she looked like. The only written detail we have

---

22. Sempronia appears at Sall., *Cat.* 25.1–5. The Fulvia who appears in the account is identified as a noblewoman (*muliere nobili, Cat.* 23.3), but Sallust provides no further details.
23. Vell. Pat. 2.74.
24. See Syme 1964, 134–6 with Syme 2016, 176–7.

FIGURE 1.2. A coin bearing Fulvia's portrait (?), *RPC* 3139 (*Bibliothèque nationale de France*).

about her physical appearance is that—at least at one point in time—one of her cheeks was swollen. This odd, not terribly helpful fact inspired a quip from the Sicilian rhetorician Sextus Clodius, who may have been a dependent of the clan to which Fulvia's first husband belonged, that she "tempted the tip of his pen," meaning that she inspired him both to write about her and to poke her face.[25]

There is a very remote possibility that Fulvia's likeness appears on several ancient coins (Figure 1.2), some of which were issued under Antonius's authority in the late 40s, when Fulvia was most fully engaged in the politics of the day.[26] The dating is less certain for some of the other coins in question. The first set of coins comes from the Roman mint at Lugdunum in Gaul (modern Lyon, France), and some of them bear Antonius's name.[27] These have been linked to a second set that was

25. Suet., *Gram. et Rhet.* 5. Sextus was a teacher of Greek and Latin with a reputation for a sharp wit. He was also a close friend of Antonius, Fulvia's last husband, with whom he liked to party. Another one of his *bon mots* was to blame his poor eyesight on his late-night drinking bouts with Antonius: all that time in dimly lit rooms did him in. Sextus also assisted Antonius in crafting his response to Cicero's first *Philippic*, the first in a series of speeches attacking Antonius that Cicero delivered in the senate. In return for Sextus's services, Cicero alleged, Antonius bestowed upon him more than 1,200 acres of land in Sextus's native Sicily (Cic., *Phil.* 2.42–3; 3.22, with commentary in Kaster 1995, 307–9 and Manuwald 2007, 406.).

26. The comprehensive assessment of the numismatic evidence is Fischer 1999, 141–68.

27. The "Fulvia" coins from Lugdunum (Crawford 1974, n. 489/5 and 489/6) are dated to 43 and 42, based on the obverse legends A(nno?) XL and A(nno?) XLI that appear with Antonius's portrait. These are generally taken to refer to his age at time of minting, but it should be noted that this would be (probably) unique among coins from the Republic. It is difficult to explain why Antonius would experiment with a dating system that smacks of Hellenistic kingship at such an early point, and why he would choose to do so at a mint in the western part of the empire. The dating of the coins from Phrygia to somewhere between 43 and 41 is reconstructed from (a) the reading of the

minted, possibly, by the city of Eumenea in Phrygia (modern Işıklı, Turkey). The connection between the two sets rests on the fact that they bear similar images of a female head in profile, usually identified as the goddess Victory (Latin, Victoria; Greek, Nike) because of the small wings that appear at the base of her neck.[28] Since the mid-nineteenth century, some scholars have asserted that the goddess has Fulvia's features,[29] and indeed the figure does look like the portrait of a real woman. Instead of idealized features and a Greek-style coiffure that usually mark an image as that of a goddess, the figure on the coins appears more like something taken from everyday life. Her hairdo, in particular, is common on representations of matrons in the late first century BCE.

Those who want to see the image as Fulvia draw further support from the fact that the Phrygian coins seem to have declared themselves as belonging to the city "of the Fulvians." This phrase is taken by some to indicate that at some point, the city of Eumenea had been renamed in Fulvia's honor—presumably in 41 or 40, when Antonius was in control of the eastern part of the Roman Empire and Fulvia was still alive. Unfortunately, the reading of the coins is uncertain: the lettering has mostly disappeared or has become illegible. Certainty is impossible, and the scenario seems highly unlikely. There is no ancient evidence that any city in Phrygia or anywhere else was renamed for Fulvia. In fact, there is no evidence for renaming a city after a living Roman woman until well into the imperial period. Furthermore, it is difficult to see what benefit there would have been for Antonius to put Fulvia on his coins in Phrygia or in Gaul. One scholar posits that it was Fulvia who pushed

---

legend "of the Fulvians," (b) the knowledge that Antonius was in the east during that period, and (c) the fact that Fulvia was still alive.

28. The ultimate source for the identification of Eumenea as the site of the mint appears to be Maximilian Borrell's 1852 catalogue for the extensive coin collection of his late brother, H. P. Borrell, a well-known figure in the antiquities trade (on whom see Kagan 2015; Waddington 1853, 149–50). The younger Borrell's argument rests on the fact that one of the coins bears the name of a magistrate, Smertorix (or Zmertorix), and this same Celtic name appears on a later coin definitely minted in Eumenea during the reign of Tiberius. While Smertorix is an uncommon name, it is worth noting that it and other names containing the onomastic element *smert-/zmert-* are found elsewhere in Galatia and throughout the Greek world (Sims-Williams 2013, 41) and in inscriptions from Gaul.

29. This, too, seems to have originated with Borrell (1852, 51 n. 457), and it has since been accepted by the majority of scholars who have written on the subject. As will become clear, I side with the skeptics, including Head 1906, 213; Babcock 1965, 12 n. 23; Mattingly 1960, 72 n. 2; and Delia 1991, 202.

her husband to give her this unprecedented honor.[30] But for that, too, there is no evidence.

If the image on these coins is indeed modeled on a real living woman, it is more probably one of the women Antonius married after Fulvia's death, Octavia, the sister of Antonius's sometime ally Octavian, or (far less likely) Cleopatra, for whom Antonius left Octavia. Portraits of both these women appear on coins several years after the "Fulvia" coins are thought to have been issued. Cleopatra appears on some of Antonius's coins minted in the east: her profile portrait appears on the reverse of a coin bearing his image on the front; she is clearly identified by the legend "Cleopatra, Queen of kings and the sons of kings." Octavia's portrait is never identified by her name (as befits a properly modest Roman woman), but the identification of her portrait rests on fairly strong, albeit circumstantial, evidence. Each portrait appears on the reverse of a coin whose front (obverse) bears a portrait either of Octavian or of Antonius, and all of them can be dated to the period between 40 and 36 BCE, when Octavia played a prominent role in keeping the alliance between her new husband and her brother from disintegrating. Octavia always appears as a mortal woman in profile, and she always wears a hairstyle identical to that borne by "Fulvia" on the earlier coins.[31] In the end, agnosticism about whether or not Fulvia appears on coins minted in the 40s BCE seems the wisest course.

Fulvia was born at her father's estate in the town of Tusculum, where the Fulvii had been prominent for generations. A midwife probably delivered the baby (Roman doctors did not generally attend births). The infant would then have been turned over to a wet-nurse, most likely a slave, who reared her through her first two years, as was common in aristocratic Roman households. In some cases, wet-nurses stayed on for years beyond weaning their charges, so Fulvia may have had the same nurse for her entire childhood. If not, the wet-nurse would have been replaced by another suitable slave: our sources say that the best nurses spoke good Greek, so that they could begin a child's education as early as possible.[32] Upper-class Romans were expected to be bilingual in Greek and Latin. Sempronia and Bambalio will have spent time with

---

30. Kleiner 1992, 361.
31. A good summary of the issues around the numismatic portraits of Antonius's wives can be found in Woods 1999, 41–51.
32. Soranus 2. 19; Rawson 2003, 122–3.

their daughter, but most of Fulvia's early childhood will have been spent in the care of her nurse.

Fulvia's nurse, like the nurses we see in ancient literature, probably told her charge stories to keep her entertained and made sure that she had an assortment of toys with which to entertain herself. Roman children played with many of the same toys that children use today: rattles, dolls, spinning tops, child-sized pushcarts, and balls are often found in archaeological excavations at Roman sites or are depicted in Roman art. Perhaps the young Fulvia rode around the garden in a miniature wagon pulled by a goat or sheep. She likely had some pets, too, since there was room for them at a country house. Ponies, dogs, assorted birds (including geese, ducks, and doves), and rabbits were common companions for wealthy children.[33] Her human playmates likely included children from neighboring estates, visiting cousins, and slave children being raised in her parents' household. Whether or not Fulvia grew up alongside her older half-brother, Natta, will have depended in large part on how Sempronia's first marriage ended. If she and her husband divorced, their son is unlikely to have moved with his mother to Tusculum. Children of divorced Roman parents generally resided with their fathers.[34] If, however, Sempronia had become a widow, then Natta and Fulvia may have spent many hours together.

Around the age of seven, Roman girls began their formal education. Rich young ladies like Fulvia had slave tutors (called *paedagogi* or *didaskaloi*) to teach them at home, rather than going to school outside the house. After learning to read, young girls spent their time with morally edifying texts, mostly epic poetry and a selection of dramas that were not too scandalous. A young woman might even learn to sing and dance, but only to a point. Too much of that sort of thing was unseemly; she might become like the conspirator Sempronia. Some young ladies might also study philosophy or rhetoric, if they showed aptitude and if their fathers encouraged it. But most steered clear of these more manly pursuits, as Fulvia probably did. Excessive education could render a girl unmarriageable, and getting married was supposed to be every Roman woman's goal. A young lady's studies ought to instill a sense of propriety and bestow upon her some refinement and an appreciation for literature. Her education was not intended to sharpen her mind, but rather

---

33. Bradley 1998.
34. The evidence suggests this was the general circumstance, rather than a hard and fast rule. See Evans Grubbs 2005.

to fashion her into a woman who was dutiful and affectionate with her parents, a careful manager of her household, and supportive of her husband.

So far, we have reconstructed Fulvia's early life based on what we know generally about growing up in an aristocratic Roman family and the education of Roman girls. With a single exception, it is difficult to pinpoint anything about her early life that might have shaped her into the formidable woman she became. The one specific thing we know about Fulvia's early years that may have encouraged her to become exceptionally self-reliant is that at some point, she watched her family splinter. We do not know if this happened through divorce or her father's death, but it seems clear that his involvement in her life lessened greatly, if it did not disappear altogether. If Bambalio did indeed die prematurely, that would explain why Sempronia's next husband, Murena, took on at least one major paternal duty. He arranged his teenaged stepdaughter's first marriage to one of his political allies and close friends, Publius Clodius Pulcher. If Bambalio and Sempronia merely divorced, however, the situation must have been more complicated. Bambalio would still, by tradition, have been expected to be in charge of making such an arrangement, and his approval would be required before the union could move forward. But given the difference between his social standing and that of Murena, a decorated soldier, former provincial governor, and the consul of 62, Bambalio would hardly have been in a position to raise a strong objection to a match that Murena and Sempronia pushed for, even if he wanted to. Regardless of who arranged Fulvia's engagement to Clodius, the marriage set her on a path that put her on the pages of our history books.

2

Fulvia Enters the Scene

We have so far reconstructed Fulvia's lineage and what her early years might have been like, but we have not yet seen much of Fulvia herself. As is often the case for Roman women, the ancient sources are silent about Fulvia until her first marriage, to Publius Clodius Pulcher. This was a surprising match, but it also seems to have been a happy one until it came to an abrupt end. Clodius's death ultimately resulted in Fulvia's entanglement in one of the most momentous events of the 50s BCE.

The In-Laws

At the tail-end of the 60s, when she was in her mid-to-late teens, Fulvia married Publius Clodius, a scion of what was arguably the most prestigious clan in Rome at that time, the *gens Claudia*. Despite the clout that came with being a Claudius, Clodius preferred the more fashionable spelling of his clan name, as did at least two of his sisters and, possibly, one of his brothers. The rest of the family, including Clodius's children, opted for the traditional form.[1] While it is entirely possible that the union of Clodius and Fulvia was a genuine love match, that is unlikely to have been a primary motivating factor in their decision to marry. Romantic feelings were normally only of secondary importance in the careful calculus made by Roman aristocratic families in selecting mates for their children—sons as well as daughters. Far more weight was

---

1. Riggsby 2002, 117–9 and Tatum 1999, 247–8. It was long thought that Clodius used the popular spelling of his family name to encourage voters to see him as a "man of the people," but the earliest appearance of the name in a series of letters from Cicero to his friend Atticus predates by at least two years Clodius's efforts to obtain plebeian status and the tribunate.

Fulvia. Celia E. Schultz, Oxford University Press. © Oxford University Press 2021.
DOI: 10.1093/oso/9780190697136.003.0002

given to factors like the prospective spouse's family's rank, and his or her own connections, wealth, moral character, physical appearance, and, for men, potential for a successful political career.

Within Rome's elite, rank was determined not primarily by wealth and education (both of which the Claudii had in plenty), although those certainly counted. What really mattered was the military glory and political offices achieved by the men of the family. Clodius belonged to one of two patrician branches of the *gens Claudia* (Figure 2.1), both of which were descended from sons of the famous censor of the late fourth century BCE, Appius Claudius Caecus ("the Blind"). The senior line—to which Clodius belonged—used the *cognomen* Pulcher ("beautiful/handsome"); the junior branch distinguished themselves from their cousins by calling themselves Nero, an old Sabine word related to Latin *fortis*, "strong."[2] Between them, these two branches of the clan were able to maintain for several centuries an unmatched dominance of Roman politics and society. By the end of the Republic, they had between them achieved twenty-eight consulships, five dictatorships, seven censorships, six triumphs (a parade celebrating a major military victory), and two ovations, a lesser form of military honor.[3] Even Cicero, who never had an easy relationship with any member of the clan, heaps superlatives on the men in the family, calling them "most noble and distinguished people . . . the most courageous men."[4]

Many Claudii were famous; some were infamous. The most villainous member of the clan was Appius Claudius the Decemvir, so called because of his service on the Board of Ten Men (*decemviri*) who established Rome's first law code in 451–450 BCE. His crime was to arrange to have a virtuous, freeborn young woman named Verginia falsely identified as a slave so that he could have his way with her. Her father killed her rather than allow her to submit to the Decemvir's lust.[5] Another Claudius, as consul in 249 during the First Carthaginian War, failed to honor the gods properly and as a result lost an entire fleet at the Sicilian

---

2. Suet., *Tib.* 1.2; Ernout and Meillet 1967, 438–9, s.v. *nero*.
3. Suet., *Tib.* 1.2. The first three items in this list are political offices. The consulship was the most powerful regular office in the Republic. The dictatorship, which superseded the consulship, was a position that could be created by the Senate to respond to a specific crisis (mostly military threats). The censorship, an office elected only once every five years, came with the power to conduct the census of Roman citizens, to revise the senatorial membership, and to award highly lucrative contracts for public works.
4. *Cael.* 68.
5. The most famous accounts are Livy 3.44.1–54.15 and Dion. Hal., *Ant. Rom.* 11.28.1–39.7.

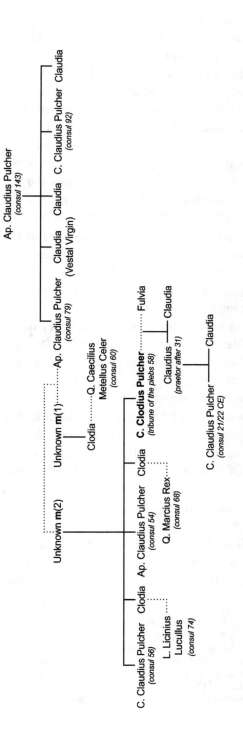

FIGURE 2.1. The *gens Claudia* (J. Jeffs).

port of Drepanum. The story is that his troubles began when he sought the gods' approval before sailing off into battle by watching the sacred chickens for a positive sign. If the gods endorsed his plan, the chickens would gobble up their food. But when the chickens refused to eat—a dire sign indeed!—Claudius became angry and threw the birds into the sea, shouting, "Since they won't eat, let them drink!"[6] A storm destroyed the fleet shortly thereafter. The moral of the story is that if you do not hear the gods the first time, they will speak more loudly the second time.

Not to be outdone, Claudian women (all of whom were, of course, called Claudia) hold prominent places in Roman history, too. For example, the sister of the man who lost the fleet at Drepanum proved just as hotheaded and arrogant as her brother. Three years after his disaster, she was returning home from an evening out and grew angry at the crowds in the street that blocked her way. Her aggravation reached such a level that she was heard to say that she wished her brother had lost more people at Drepanum so the streets would not be so crowded. City magistrates levied a heavy fine for her offending remarks.[7]

Perhaps the most notorious woman from the entire history of the Roman Republic was Clodia Metelli, one of Fulvia's sisters-in-law. She was a leader among Rome's fashionable set and was married to the consul of 60, Quintus Caecilius Metellus Celer. One of his letters to Cicero survives: Metellus comes across as a real stuffed shirt—pompous, self-righteous, and thin-skinned. The marriage was, at least in its last few years, not a happy one. Husband and wife disagreed over Clodius, Clodia's younger brother, whose efforts to advance his political career were being thwarted by Metellus. Fortunately for Clodius, Metellus died unexpectedly after the end of his consulship. At first no one even hinted that it was an unnatural death. But three years later, Cicero insinuated that Clodia had poisoned him.[8]

Cicero's claim about Metellus's death illustrates the most salient feature of the notoriety attached to any ancient Roman woman: it has less to do with any actions she actually took and more to do with the fact that

---

6. Claudius's wit is central to the story: Livy, *Per.* 19; Cic., *Nat. D.* 2.7, *Div.* 2.20; Val. Max. 1.4.3; Suet., *Tib.* 2.2. The tale, minus the dramatic bits, is also recounted in Polyb. 1.49–52.

7. Aul. Gell. 10.6.2; Suet., *Tib.* 2.3; Livy, *Per.* 19; Val. Max., 8.1.Damn.4.

8. Metellus's letter to Cicero and Cicero's response: *Fam.* 5.1 and 2 = *SBF* 1 and 2. Clodia disagrees with Metellus about her brother: Cic., *Att.* 2.1.5 = *SBA* 21.5. I follow Shackleton Bailey (*ad loc.*) in understanding *eos* to refer to Clodius and Clodia. Cicero insinuated that Clodia murdered Metellus in his speech defending her former lover against charges that he tried to poison her (*Cael.* 59–60).

she attracted the attention of an important writer of her day. Clodia, in fact, attracted the attention of two such men: the poet Catullus and the statesman Cicero. Because they focused their attention on her and wrote about her extensively, we feel like we know something about Clodia in much the same way we feel we know something about Fulvia, another of Cicero's favorite targets. In reality, of course, much of what we know about Clodia and Fulvia is not actually about the women themselves. What we know is a lot about how some prominent men portrayed them. Catullus recorded the ups and downs of his affair with Clodia in his poems, where she is called by the cryptonym "Lesbia." She is alternately intoxicatingly desirable and frustratingly fickle, if not outright cruel.[9] Cicero, who had never been a fan of Clodia, defended in court a friend of his who had once been her lover. The man, Caelius, was accused of attempting to murder Clodia. Cicero's defense speech, the *Pro Caelio* (On Behalf of Caelius), a classic of Roman invective, is a sustained assault on Clodia's moral character. The best defense is a good offense.

Other Claudias were famous for more noble reasons. One positive exemplar was Claudia Quinta ("Number Five") who, in 204 BCE during the waning days of Rome's war with Hannibal, famously welcomed the goddess known as the Great Mother (Magna Mater) to Rome from the goddess's hometown of Pergamon in Asia minor. When the barge carrying the large stone that was the Great Mother's terrestrial manifestation ran aground as it came up the Tiber river, Claudia stepped forward and not only freed the barge, but she hauled it all the way to Rome—thus disproving those who claimed she was a woman of loose morals.[10] Her moment of triumph is depicted on an altar set up in Rome by another Claudia, probably a freedwoman, more than two hundred years later (Figure 2.2). Another Claudia, some sixty years after the Great Mother arrived in Rome, used the sanctity of her priesthood—she was a Vestal Virgin—to protect her father, the consul of 143. He claimed the right to a triumphal procession in honor of his recent victory over the tribe of the Salassi.[11] When the senate declined to award him the honor,

---

9. Clodia has long fascinated scholars, and she has recently been the subject of a full-length biography by Skinner (2011). Scholars distinguish her from her two sisters by the epithet Metelli ("belonging to Metellus"), a reference to her husband, but it should be noted that a Roman woman's legal name was not altered upon her marriage.

10. The earliest references to this story are found in two of Cicero's public attacks on Clodia Metelli (*Cael.* 34 and *Har. Resp.* 27). More elaborate accounts are found in Livy (29.10–14) and Ovid (*Fast.* 4.180–372). Leach 2007 explores the relationship between the literary sources and Claudia Syntyche's altar.

11. Cic., *Cael.* 34; Val. Max. 5.4.6; Suet., *Tib.* 2.4.

FIGURE 2.2. Altar set up by Claudia Syntyche, Museo Capitolino, Rome.
Source: B. Malter, http://arachne.uni-koeln.de/item/objekt/16367.

he proceeded with the parade anyway. To prevent anyone from forcibly pulling him from his chariot as he rode through the city, Claudia rode alongside him. The legend was such a point of pride that in 41 BCE, when one of her relatives chose the artwork for coins produced by the mint under his direction, he chose to put her on the reverse (Figure 2.3).

Fulvia's in-laws, then, were an illustrious bunch; her own family was far less prominent. As we discussed in the previous chapter, none of men in her branch of either her mother's or her father's family had achieved high office since her maternal great-grandfather's consulship in 129. They had not been prominent in so long that Cicero, himself a political outsider because no one in his family had reached the consulship before his own in 63, could dismiss Fulvia's father as a man of "no account."[12] Given the discrepancy in status between their families, the

12. *Phil.* 3.16.

FIGURE 2.3. Denarius of C. Clodius Vestalis, *RRC* 512/2.
Source: Yale University Art Gallery, 2001.87.2160.

union of Fulvia and Clodius invites further contemplation. In the end, scandal as much as anything else seems to have brought them together.

Clodius

Clodius was born in approximately 92 BCE, the youngest son in a brood of six adult siblings: three brothers and three sisters.[13] Their father, Appius Claudius (consul of 79), died prematurely in 76, when Clodius was in his mid-teens. This left Clodius's oldest brother, also named Appius and then in his early twenties, as the head of the household. The young Appius proved himself a capable *paterfamilias* by launching careers for himself and his younger brothers and finding desirable marriages for two of his sisters; one of the sisters was already married when their father passed away. If their father's death had an adverse effect on the family's financial standing, as has sometimes been argued, their difficulties were soon remedied.[14] There is strong evidence that within a decade, family finances were fine. At Rome, politics was a rich man's occupation, and all three brothers went on to successful political careers. Public office in Rome did not come with a salary, and campaigns were—then, as now—expensive. Clodius's three sisters married the consuls of 74, 68, and 60—some of the most powerful men of the day.

---

13. Tatum 1999 offers a full-length biography.
14. A passage in Varro (*Rust.* 3.16.2), where the character of the younger Appius Claudius says that his family's poverty was remedied by the generosity of his brother-in-law Lucullus, was long taken as a straightforward statement. Tatum has argued, however, that it is joke (1992, 36): Lucullus was famously parsimonious. Yet the case is still not closed. Treggiari (1991, 110) notes that marriages between cousins (as was the case for Lucullus's and Metellus's marriage to two of Appius's sisters) can be a sign that the women involved had insufficient dowries, or none at all.

The complicated and fast-paced world of politics in late republican Rome was not a place for the faint of heart nor the high-minded. Fortunately for them, the Claudius brothers were not encumbered by either timidity or lofty principles. When the three of them came onto the political scene in the 60s and early 50s, it was a period of great upheaval and contention, of the increasing politicization of the urban masses, and of rampant electoral bribery and political violence. It was not unusual for a politician, in a public assembly, to have his supporters physically threaten a colleague who disagreed with him.[15] The age was also characterized by deep political divisions among Rome's leaders. These were rarely motivated by ideological differences. Groups of politicians worked together to obtain power and to curb the influence of their opponents, and sometimes their efforts benefited the people of Rome. But the welfare of the state was not necessarily, in those days, foremost in the minds of these men who sought glory and political supremacy for themselves.

In this corrupt political environment, the Claudii thrived. Appius was consul in 54 and, despite having been caught up in a rather spectacular electoral scandal while in office (see p. 41), he reached the censorship four years later. In between these two offices, he governed the province of Cilicia (in Asia minor) with exceptional rapacity and viciousness. As the competition between Pompey and Caesar ratcheted up through the decade of the 50s, Appius allied himself with Pompey, a relationship cemented by the marriage of one of Appius's daughters to one of Pompey's sons. We can reconstruct something of Appius's personality through Cicero's letters. Although none of Appius's letters to Cicero survives, thirteen letters to him by the orator are preserved, and he is mentioned in several letters to other people. Appius comes across as a man of exceptional arrogance—even among Roman aristocrats—who easily took umbrage at relatively minor offenses. Cicero coined the term *Appietas* ("the quality of being an Appius") for his haughtiness.[16] The personality and career of the middle brother, Gaius, are less well attested. He achieved the praetorship in 56, but his career ended

---

15. Lintott 1968, 68–88.
16. *Appietas*: Cic., *Fam.* 3.7.5 = SBF 71.5. The letters to Appius comprise the third book of *Epistulae ad Familiares* (= SBF 64–76). That others shared Cicero's opinion is made clear by letters to Cicero from his friends. For example, Caelius (Cic., *Fam.* 8.12.1–4 = SBF 98) calls Appius ungrateful, greedy, and an ape. See also Cic., *Fam.* 5.10a.2 = SBF 259.2. The bribery scandal is described in Cic., *Att.* 4.17.2–3 = SBA 91.2–3. Cicero, who succeeded Appius as the governor of Cilicia, reports the damage Appius had done to province in *Att.* 5.16.2 = SBA 109.2.

with a conviction for financial mismanagement of the province of Asia, where he served as governor from 55 to 53.[17] The youngest was, of course, Clodius. He was exceptionally popular with urban non-elites, serving as tribune of plebs in 58 and, further up the political ladder, as aedile in 56. He had his supporters among the wealthy as well.

But we are getting ahead of the story. In the mid-60s, Clodius had not yet held elected office. He had, however, already acquired a reputation as a dangerous opponent and as someone willing to overturn the status quo for his own benefit.[18] As did many other young, aristocratic gentlemen, he began his career with military service, an essential prerequisite for public office. It is not entirely clear when Clodius joined the staff of his brother-in-law, L. Licinius Lucullus, but it is likely that Clodius departed for the east with Lucullus when he set out, late in 74 or early the next year, to lead Rome's war against Mithridates, king of Pontus on the southern coast of the Black Sea. Clodius would then have been about eighteen years of age, just right for a first campaign. Appius went along, too. We do not know if Gaius joined them, although that seems likely. It was an opportunity too good to pass up: the war promised to be a glamorous and lucrative exploit.[19]

Instead it turned out to be grueling and slow. After five years of hard fighting, Lucullus had all but brought the war to a close, but his efforts in the year 68 did not go well. An invasion of northern Armenia had not enticed Mithridates to a pitched battle, and the early onset of winter weather added to the Romans' growing frustration and displeasure. When the troops refused to follow Lucullus further north, he was forced to march southward toward the city of Nisibis (the modern Turkish city of Nusaybin on the Syrian border). While they wintered there, Clodius chafed at Lucullus's disregard for him and nursed his jealousy over the plum assignments handed to Appius.[20] By early in 67, Clodius saw an opportunity to undercut his brother-in-law: the rank-and-file were already unhappy with their commander, and news coming from Rome indicated that Lucullus was about to be relieved of his command, rendering him largely impotent in the face of opposition. Encouraging the men to call him "the soldiers' friend," Clodius incited a mutiny. Lucullus

---

17. Caelius wrote to Cicero about the affair: Cic., *Fam.* 8.8.2 = *SBF* 84.2.
18. Sall., *Hist.* 5.12; Plut, *Vit. Luc.* 34.1; Cass. Dio 36.14.4.
19. The most extensive ancient sources for this episode are Plut., *Vit. Luc.* 32.1–35.7 and Cass. Dio 36.14.1–17.3.
20. Plut., *Vit. Luc.* 21.1.

held onto his command only a little while longer. He was replaced by Pompey, who would finally bring the war to a victorious conclusion, but even he could not end the conflict until 63.

Somehow Clodius emerged from his first act of insubordination entirely unscathed. He deserted Lucullus and took up a position on the staff of another brother-in-law, Q. Marcius Rex, who had been consul at Rome in 68 and was then governor of the province of Cilicia, just east and south of Lucullus's province.[21] Clodius clearly had a better relationship with Marcius, who immediately put him to work in his campaign to crush the pirate fleets that had been ravaging coastal communities and disrupting marine commerce across the Mediterranean. This was no small task. Rather than the individual ships that modern audiences are used to seeing on movie screens, these pirates commanded entire fleets of warships and were able to sack large cities, including many on the coasts of Italy and Sicily.[22] When threatened, the pirates often retreated into the mountains of Cilicia, and now Marcius was charged with fighting them on both land and sea.

Clodius was given command of a fleet, a prominent assignment that our sources say he owed more to his kinship with the commander than with any actual experience or competence in naval warfare. He was soon caught by the pirates, who demanded ransom money. For help, Clodius turned to the king of Cyprus, who responded with only a paltry sum—at least to Clodius's way of thinking. Clodius would wait a long time for revenge. Nearly a decade later, as tribune of the plebs, Clodius would put forward a bill that called for the annexation of Cyprus as a province of Rome. But for now, the whole kidnapping episode was doubly mortifying: he had been caught and he was not worth a sufficiently impressive ransom. The pirates eventually released Clodius, and Marcius gave him another opportunity to prove himself by sending him to assist the king of Syria in his ongoing conflict with local Arab leaders. Holding true to form, once in the capital of Antioch, Clodius stirred up unrest (no other details are preserved). This time, he barely escaped with his life.[23]

---

21. Cass. Dio 36.17.2–3.

22. The pirates were brazen enough to attack Ostia, near Rome at the mouth of the Tiber river, as well as major ports at Misenum in Campania and Brundisium on Italy's southernmost Adriatic coast. For a survey of Roman interaction with the pirates in this period, see de Souza 1999, 99–178.

23. Cic., *Har. resp.* 42; App., *B. Civ.* 2.23; Cass. Dio 36.17.3 and 38.30.5. Clodius also arranged that the new province of Cyprus be assigned to his political enemy, Cato. By removing Cato from politics in the capital, the law settled two of Clodius's scores at once.

After this third embarrassment, it was time to return home. Once back in Rome, Clodius set about making a name for himself in the law courts, where he gained renown as an exceptionally powerful orator.[24] His most prominent case, undertaken in the summer of 65, was the prosecution of Catiline, the future leader of the unsuccessful conspiracy to overthrow the government that we discussed in the previous chapter. In 65, however, the case against Catiline was somewhat less dramatic. His troubles stemmed from allegations brought to Rome from Africa, where he had been serving as governor. The provincials were so upset by Catiline's behavior that delegations arrived in Rome even before his term had come to end. Cicero was willing to defend Catiline, even though he expected a guilty verdict. In the end, however, Cicero did not take up the case. Catiline still managed to avoid conviction; some years later, Cicero would allege that this was because Clodius, as prosecutor, had colluded with the defense.[25] The accusation cannot be proved.

Clodius's personal life was at least as interesting as his professional endeavors. He was very much a man-about-town. Although no physical likeness of him survives from antiquity, he is reported to have been handsome and stylish. Cicero snidely punned on Clodius's original cognomen, *pulcher*, calling him *pulchellus* ("pretty boy") in several letters to his friend Atticus. With great disdain, Cicero described him as *urbanissimus* ("very refined").[26] Clodius liked to keep a retinue of Greeks with him—a sure sign of decadent luxury, at least in the eyes of Rome's moralists.[27] He also had a rakish reputation and hobnobbed with Rome's smart set, at the center of which was his sister Clodia, the wife of Metellus.[28] Two of his close associates would play prominent roles later in Fulvia's life. One was the younger Gaius Scribonius Curio, whose father (of the same name) later served as Clodius's defense attorney. Curio seems to have been, like Clodius, a man of excessive refinement and faddish tastes. The other was Curio's close friend, Marcus Antonius, who would be famous for centuries as the associate of Caesar and the lover of

---

24. Vell. Pat. 2.45.1; Tac., *Ann.* 11.7; Plut., *Vit. Caes.* 9.1. Even Cicero, who was certainly not a fan, could admit in at least one instance that Clodius had delivered a "really eloquent" speech (*sane diserto, Att.* 4.15.4 = SBA 90.4).

25. Accusations against Catiline: Sall., *Cat.* 18.3; Cic., *Cael.* 10. Strength of the case against him: Cic. *Att.* 1.1.1 and 1.2.1 = SBA 10.1 and 11.1. Possible collusion: Cic., *Har. resp.* 42; Asconius, 66, 85, and 89C.

26. *Att.* 1.16.10, 2.1.4, 2.18.3, 2.22.1 = SBA 16.10, 21.4, 38.3, 42.1; *Cael.* 36.

27. Cic., *Mil.* 28.

28. Cic., *Cael.* 36.

Cleopatra. Clodius and Antonius appear to have had a falling out later in their careers, although the extent of the disagreement and its cause are difficult to reconstruct. Regardless, Antonius proved himself a loyal friend in the end.[29]

Within Clodius's circle of friends was the poet and orator C. Licinius Calvus, famous for his spare style of speaking and for scandalous verses about some of the most powerful men of the day, including Pompey and Caesar.[30] Less warm was Clodius's relationship with Calvus's friend Catullus,[31] the most important poet of their generation and, as we have already mentioned, one of Clodia's lovers. Catullus felt he had to compete with Clodius for her attention, as he revealed in Poem 79, where he puns on the family cognomen and calls Clodius "Lesbius," the proper pseudonym for the brother of a woman called Lesbia: "Lesbius is handsome (*pulcher*), and why shouldn't he be? Lesbia prefers him to you, Catullus, and your whole family. . . ." Catullus perhaps insinuates an incestuous relationship between the siblings. Just how close brother and sister were was also a favorite topic for Cicero, who repeatedly alleged that they crossed the line from emotionally close to physically intimate. The rumor, in fact, is repeated by other sources and is said about Clodius with all three of his sisters. Yet there is no indication that the accusation was based on any actual evidence.[32] Such claims were not uncommon in Roman political invective: Cicero himself was the target of a similar accusation about his relationship with his daughter.[33] In a society without libel laws, one could say anything one wanted in a public venue without fear of repercussions.

After some time in Rome, Clodius spent the years 64–63 serving on the staff of the governor of Transalpine Gaul, Lucius Licinius Murena, whom he knew from the time they had both served with Lucullus in the war against Mithridates. Murena seems to have been a successful governor, and Clodius, for once, behaved himself while on Murena's

---

29. The younger Curio: Cic., *Att.* 1.14.5 = SBA 14.5. Antonius: Cic., *Mil.* 40; *Phil.* 2.21 and 48–9; Plut., *Vit. Ant.* 2.4.

30. Tatum 1999, 82–5, and Wiseman 1968, 297–9. For a summary of what we know of Calvus's life and works (none of which survives except in the most fragmentary state), see P. L. Schmidt, *BNP*, s.v. "Licinius I.31" with bibliography.

31. Calvus appears in several of Catullus's poems (no. 14, 50, 53, and 96), and the two poets are sometimes paired, as in Hor., *Sat.* 1.10.19 and Ov., *Am.* 3.9.61–2.

32. See also Cic., *Mil* 73; Plut., *Vit. Luc.* 38.1, *Vit. Cic.* 29.4–5.

33. The tradition is preserved in later sources, including a diatribe against Cicero, wrongly attributed to Sallust (Ps.-Sall., *Inv. in Cic.* 2) and Cass. Dio 46.18.

staff.[34] At the end of his term in Gaul, Murena and his entourage returned to the capital in mid-63. The former governor then stood for the consulship of 62; Clodius helped with the campaign—probably by distributing the bribes that were now an almost expected (but still illegal) part of any political campaign.[35] Murena's candidacy received a further boost from a small but important gesture on the part of his cousin Licinia, a Vestal Virgin. It was customary for the priestesses of Vesta to sit together at public entertainments. At one particular gladiatorial show, after the crowd had been seated, Licinia made a show of standing up to relinquish her seat to Murena. The image of Murena seated among the priestesses would have made quite an impression; it was a strong endorsement of his personal character.[36] It is likely that at this time, as Clodius worked closely with Murena, that Fulvia, Murena's stepdaughter, caught his attention.

Immediately after Murena was elected, he was accused of electoral bribery by one of his unsuccessful competitors. For the trial, held in the autumn before he was to take office, Murena arranged an all-star defense team, including the two most prominent orators of the day: Q. Hortensius Hortalus, Cicero, who was still in office as one of the consuls of 63, and Murena's cousin Crassus, who had not yet formed his informal alliance with Pompey and Caesar. The team of advocates secured Murena's acquittal.

Murena's year in office began with the final suppression of Catiline's conspiracy on a battlefield near the city of Pistoia, about 200 miles north of Rome. Much of the rest of the year was taken up with speculation and anxiety about what would happen when Pompey finally returned from his wildly successful military campaigns in the east. He had been out there since he took over the war against Mithridates in 66. His successes over the last few years meant that Pompey was now, without question, the most powerful man in Rome. Would he march his army on Rome and seize control for himself, as the dictator Sulla had done twenty years

---

34. Murena's service with Lucullus: Cic., *Mur.* 20. Tatum rightly points out that Cicero's effusive praise of Murena's governorship in this speech gives the lie to his later accusation (*Har. resp.* 42) of Clodius's criminal activities in Gaul: "Clodius, who continued in Murena's good books, can scarcely have been a renegade under so upright a governor. In the matter of his Gallic service, there is no reason to take Cicero's charges against Clodius seriously," (1999, 56).

35. See Tatum 1999, 58 n. 149, and Crawford's commentary on Cic., *In Clod. et Cur.* F11 Crawford (1994, 250).

36. Cic., *Mur.* 73 with DiLuzio 2016, 231–2.

before? Or would he disband his army and return home, subordinate to the will of the senate? The second option was closer to what actually happened, although Pompey never truly bent to the senate's demands.

During the summer of 62, Clodius was elected to his first public office, the quaestorship, for the year 61. No one was elected to the consulship because the mood in the city was too volatile to hold any more elections. There were still no consuls in office by mid-winter, when the capital was rocked by scandal.

Every December, the most prominent women of Rome, including the chaste priestesses of Vesta (the Vestal Virgins), gathered at the home of one of the year's leading magistrates to celebrate an overnight ritual in honor of the goddess known as Bona Dea ("the Good Goddess"). The house would be decorated with vines and twigs, and the men of the household, including the magistrate himself and his male slaves, were sent away for the evening. So comprehensive was the ban on anything male that every portrait bust and statue of a male figure in the house was to be covered over. Once the men were gone, the Vestals led the women in the sacrifice of a pig, and the evening included music and dance.[37]

In December 62, the ritual was hosted by Pompeia, the wife of Caesar, who was praetor that year. The evening began normally. Caesar and the male staff left the house as was required. Pompeia received her guests, including her mother-in-law, Aurelia, and her sister-in-law, Julia. Sempronia, Fulvia's mother, was probably there, too: as the wife of one of the sitting consuls, she surely counted among the leading ladies of Rome. As the last guest arrived, the doors were closed, and the festivities began. Since part of the household staff was off for the night, Pompeia's own slaves were assisted by a few additional women, including musicians, all slaves who had been borrowed or rented for the event. The hustle and bustle of the evening's activity and the introduction of new staff made it fairly easy for an unknown harp-player, presenting herself as one of the company of musicians brought in for the night, to slip into the house. When one of the other servants asked her to identify herself, she answered in a disturbingly deep voice. Pandemonium ensued.

Cicero summed things up in a letter to his friend Atticus: "I think you've heard that Publius Clodius, the son of Appius, was caught dressed as a woman in the house of Gaius Caesar at the public sacrifice,

---

37. The literary sources for the goddess's worship are collected in Brouwer 1989, 144–228. See especially Plut., *Quaest. Rom.* 20 and *Vit. Caes.* 9.1–10.10.

and that he was saved by a slave-girl and escaped. It really is a remarkably scandalous affair."[38] For once, Cicero cannot be accused of overstatement. It appears that at some point before the Bona Dea's ritual, Pompeia had caught Clodius's eye, but they had not yet found a way to be alone. So Clodius, with the help of one of Pompeia's slaves named Habra, had snuck into the house that night. He knew Caesar would be out, but he had failed to reckon on Aurelia, Caesar's mother, a woman renowned for her upright propriety.[39] Hearing that a man had infiltrated the festival, Aurelia ordered the servants to lock down the house. She searched room by room until she found Clodius cowering in Habra's room. Somehow, he escaped the house. Once he was gone, the Vestals repeated the sacrifice, as Roman religious protocol demanded, and then the other attendees immediately scattered for their homes. The story spread like wildfire.

Clodius was supposed to take up his quaestorship shortly after the scandal broke. But instead of departing for Sicily, he was stuck in the city as the senate worked to figure out how to handle the situation. It was not a matter to be taken lightly. The Bona Dea's ritual was a public sacrifice, meaning its success was critical to the well-being of the state. Caesar, for his part, opted not to take Clodius to court on a charge of adultery. He was perhaps leery of Clodius's great popularity with voters in the city or, more likely, was unwilling to offend Clodius's brothers and their powerful friends. Caesar was himself a popular politician, but he was not yet the political powerhouse he would become.

Murena, still consul for a few more weeks, seems to have been able to protect his friend by keeping the scandal off the senate's agenda, but the issue was raised in the middle of January, shortly after the new consuls took office. Clodius worked hard to prevent his case from going forward, even sending in a gang of his supporters to break up a voting assembly that was deciding whether to empanel a jury.[40] His efforts were unsuccessful, and in the springtime, Clodius had to appear in court. His defense was that he could not have been in Caesar's house that night because he, Clodius, had been in Interamna, a town about 90 Roman miles from the city. His story was backed up by his close friend, C. Cassinius Schola, who came into Rome to testify. Schola's testimony, however, was

---

38. Cic., *Att.* 1.12.3 = *SBA* 12.3.
39. At least according to Plut., *Vit. Caes.* 9.3.
40. Cic., *Att.* 1.14.5 = *SBA* 14.5.

countered by Aurelia and Julia, who were adamant that they had seen Clodius in the house. Another witness also undermined Clodius's alibi. Cicero testified that he had, in fact, had a visit from Clodius at his house in Rome earlier on the day in question, so Clodius could not have been in Interamna. Even so, Clodius was acquitted—probably because of lavish bribes paid to the jury and because of the fear of violence threatened by Clodius's less reputable supporters.[41] As we saw earlier in the case of the king of Cyprus, Clodius was never one to forget a wrong done to him. He would nurse a grudge against Cicero for the rest of his life.[42]

So where is Fulvia in all of this? It is highly unlikely that she was already engaged or married to Clodius in the winter of 62: she is completely absent from all ancient accounts of the scandal. Even Cicero, who was certainly no fan of either Clodius or Fulvia and who liked to bring up the Bona Dea affair whenever there was an opportunity, does not mention her. She was probably at home that night, as a proper young lady ought to be. She will have heard what happened at Pompeia's house as soon as Sempronia dashed in the door.

Engagement

Clodius's history of rash, thrill-seeking behavior was, in all probability, a key factor in his willingness to marry Fulvia. The city was scandalized by the Bona Dea affair—Caesar promptly divorced his wife, saying that, even though there was no evidence of an affair, "Caesar's wife must be beyond suspicion"—and the outcome of the trial was a public embarrassment.[43] It is easy to see why, in the months that followed the winter of 62–61, Rome's most elite families were unwilling to attach their daughters to such an irreverent, unpredictable mate—even if he was a Claudius Pulcher and even if his career looked like it was off to a good start. To a family of a less elevated status, however, Clodius would still appeal. By the standards of Roman high society, Fulvia came from a moderately distinguished background, but her family's reputation had been tarnished by her grandfather's reputation for eccentricity, her father's political inactivity, and perhaps her aunt's involvement with Catiline.

---

41. Cic., *Att.* 1.16.1–11 = *SBA* 16.1–11.
42. See p. 41.
43. Plut., *Vit. Caes.* 10.8; Suet., *Iul.* 74.2; App., *B Civ.* 2.14.

Under normal circumstances, marriage into so prestigious a clan as the Claudii Pulchri would probably have been beyond Fulvia's reach, but here was a Claudius that one might get at a discount, as it were.

Fulvia's own desirability will have improved with her mother's remarriage to L. Licinius Murena, especially once he became consul in 62.[44] For Clodius in particular, marriage to Fulvia would cement his friendship and political alliance with her stepfather. She also offered exceptional wealth (Cicero reports that Clodius's own funds were depleted by bribing the jurors in the Bona Dea trial, although that is likely to be exaggeration),[45] and most critically, as an aristocratic young woman, she would offer unimpeachable virginal chastity. All this translated into respectability. One also wonders, but could never prove one way or the other, if Fulvia may have, even at this young age, shown sufficient strength of character to be a stabilizing force. Some years later, in the wake of his own scandal, Marcus Antonius married Fulvia as he sought to stabilize his own uncertain position in the city.[46] Perhaps people thought she might do the same for Clodius.

The most likely timing of Fulvia's engagement to Clodius is the brief period between his acquittal in court and his departure for Sicily: it would have been a strong statement of Murena's support for Clodius at a time when he most needed it. Another plausible option is that they were engaged shortly after he returned from the province in early 60. Either way, Clodius seems to have stayed out of trouble while abroad.[47] Any reservations troubling Murena, Sempronia, Bambalio, or even Fulvia herself were allayed by several months of good behavior on Clodius's part.

Probably during the spring of 61, Clodius met with either Murena or Bambalio (or both) to arrange a verbal contract that spelled out the terms of the betrothal, including Fulvia's dowry.[48] Tradition dictated that once the agreement was worked out, the couple sealed the arrangement with a kiss. Clodius will then have presented Fulvia with, among other gifts, a plain iron ring, a modest present believed to harken

---

44. The career of her half-brother, Lucius Pinarius Natta, seems to have benefited as well. The new prominence Murena brought him may explain, at least in part, his surprising adlection to the college of pontiffs in 58. See Babcock 1965, 8.

45. Cic., *In Clodium et Curionem*, Frag. 6a and 6b, with commentary from Crawford 1994, 246–7.

46. Plut., *Vit. Ant.* 10.2–3.

47. Even Cicero's hostile review of Clodius's career offers no criticism of his time in Sicily, preferring instead to conflate his quaestorship in Sicily with the Bona Dea episode (*Har. resp.* 43).

48. For a detailed reconstruction of Roman engagement traditions, see Treggiari 1991, 125–60.

back to Rome's early days of austerity and simplicity. The engagement would then have been celebrated with a party hosted by Fulvia's family, attended by relatives, family friends, and political allies.

While Clodius was in Sicily, Fulvia and her family were left to make arrangements for the wedding, which must have happened before Clodius took up his next office, as tribune of the plebs, in 58.[49] Roman wedding dates were carefully chosen: the Roman calendar included many days that were unpropitious for such an undertaking. Festival days, days of a sacred nature (when the law courts were also closed), and the named days of each month—the Kalends, the Nones, and Ides—all had to be avoided.

Roman weddings, especially among the well-to-do, could be lavish affairs with many guests. The event usually took place at the home of the bride's family. It began with the taking of the auspices by an *auspex*, a friend or relative designated to look for divine signs, possibly in the entrails of a sacrificial animal, that the gods approved of the marriage. The presence of a priest was not required. There would be feasting and giving of gifts—by everyone else to the couple and between the couple themselves. At the end of the evening, the bride's family dispatched their guests with gift baskets.

At some point during the festivities, the bridegroom slipped away to his own home so that he could be there to receive his bride at the end of the evening. Some of the partygoers, including a married woman who served as the *pronuba* (something akin to a matron-of-honor), escorted the bride in a joyous torch-lit procession to her new home. The partygoers joked and sang obscene songs as they went. Some threw nuts to the crowd that lined the streets to see what was going on. Upon arriving at her new home, the bride crossed the threshold and her marriage began.

Life with Clodius

Of Fulvia's marriage we know very little, except that it seems to have been a happy one. The only detail we have is that she and Clodius were rarely apart, suggesting that they enjoyed one another's company.[50] Their

---

49. Cicero implies (*Phil.* 2.48) that Clodius was already married when he took up the tribunate. On aristocratic Roman weddings, see Hersch 2010.
50. Cic., *Mil.* 28 and 55.

son Claudius[51] was born fairly early in their marriage, and a daughter, Claudia, followed a few years later.

The extent to which Fulvia was involved in Clodius's political career is subject to some debate. Some historians, swayed by the later portrait of a devious and domineering Fulvia painted for us by Antonius's political enemies in the late 40s, have argued that she was instrumental in driving Clodius forward.[52] Yet there is no real evidence to support this, and, as we saw from the moment he began his military service, Clodius needed no prodding to advance his own interests. Furthermore, it is unlikely that Fulvia, who was probably between the age of fifteen and eighteen when she married, was already the political force she was to known to be in adulthood. Of course, given what we know of her activities later in life, it is hard to believe that Fulvia, even as a young, new wife, was content merely to tend to the children, run her household, and contemplate menus and entertainments. She is much more likely to have been an eager student of the political gamesmanship that engaged her stepfather, her husband, and their friends. In this, she was not alone. As we will see, especially in the next chapters, aristocratic women did not often leave politicking entirely to the men.

Clodius's career had so far proceeded along fairly conventional lines (even if his personal behavior had not), but it veered into unusual territory in 59 when he took a rare, though not unprecedented, step. He had still not shed the opprobrium he had earned in the Bona Dea scandal, and his efforts to gain the next rung on the normal political ladder, the aedileship, seem to have been blocked. Thus Clodius cast about for an opportunity to prove himself, and he set his sights on election to a different office, that of tribune of the plebs, an office only open to plebeians. Of course, as a member of the *gens Claudia*, Clodius was a patrician, and so was banned from competing for the position. At first, Clodius tried to have himself transferred to plebeian status by popular vote. His efforts were thwarted, however, largely by his brother-in-law, Clodia's husband, Metellus. This left him one recourse: adoption into a plebeian family. There was no pretense that this adoption was about anything but politics. His adoptive father, Fonteius, was many years younger than Clodius, and Clodius, in contradiction of Roman custom, made no effort to take up his new clan name. For the adoption to be legal, it needed

---

51. The children were known by the more old-fashioned spelling of the family name. See Riggsby 2002, 117.

52. Val. Max., 3.5.3; Babcock 1965, 20–1; Marshall 1985, 167; Huzar 1985–6, 100.

to be approved in a voting assembly, and this, in turn, required the compliance and assistance of Caesar, Pompey, and Crassus to overcome the considerable senatorial opposition that had torpedoed Clodius's earlier efforts. Each member of this powerful alliance, which had been formed just the year before, clearly understood that Clodius might be a useful ally, so Caesar, as consul, pushed through Clodius's adoption.

Now free to compete for the tribunate of the year 58, Clodius campaigned on popular issues, most importantly free grain for Roman citizens. Upon election, he swiftly delivered a package of legislation that was designed to cement his growing reputation as a defender of the people. It included, among other things, the establishment of a grain dole for all Roman citizens and the restoration of neighborhood organizations called *collegia*. These had been banned some years before because of their role in civil unrest. Restoring them worked to Clodius's benefit since it legitimized one of his preferred political tools: violence. His supporters, who had already shown their willingness to fight on his behalf in the lead-up to the Bona Dea trial, remained dangerously loyal. Even Caesar and Pompey, who were, over the course of 58, increasingly displeased with Clodius's activities, steered clear of direct conflict with him.

One of the most valuable things that the tribunate gave Clodius was a platform from which he could finally pay back Cicero for testifying against him in the Bona Dea trial. Clodius whipped up popular sentiment against the former consul on the charge that Cicero had illegally put to death some of Catiline's co-conspirators in the wake of the conspiracy's revelation in 63. He drafted a bill, effective retroactively, that would exile anyone who had ever put a citizen to death without a trial. Reading the writing on the wall, Caesar offered Cicero a position on his staff in Gaul, where Caesar was about to take over as governor.[53] Cicero nobly or, rather, foolishly refused the invitation. He stood his ground against Clodius until the tribune put the bill before the people in March. Once it was voted it into law, Cicero left that night, before he could be thrown out of the city.[54] Clodius, never one to let go of a grudge, then added an amendment making Cicero's voluntary exile into an official expulsion. He was forbidden to come within

---

53. Plut., *Vit. Cic.* 30.3–4; Cass. Dio 38.15.2.
54. Cic., *Sest.* 53–54.

400 miles of Italy, and anyone who helped Cicero to return would be put to death.[55]

By the time Clodius's tribunate came to an end in December 58, he had wrecked his relationship with Pompey, still the most powerful man in Rome, especially now that Caesar was up in Gaul; Crassus had been sidelined by his two allies shortly after they joined forces.[56] Although Clodius had benefited from the support of the Three in his efforts to obtain the tribuneship, he had begun to position himself as a competitor—mostly of Pompey—a few months into his time in office. His main target was Pompey's eastern settlement, the very thing that had launched Pompey into a position of unparalleled power and had made him the target of senatorial opposition. The dissolution of the friendship between Clodius and Pompey over the course of 58 allowed Pompey, in the following year, to swing his support behind Cicero, whose own allies had never ceased to work for his return. Clodius was not in office that year, but he continued to wield power through his armed supporters, who repeatedly attempted to derail efforts to recall the orator. In one instance they started a riot during an assembly to vote on a proposal to end Cicero's exile. Assisted by a band of gladiators provided by Clodius's brother, Appius, they drove off one of the tribunes who was putting the measure before the crowd. Then, after they had attacked the crowd itself, they went "with swords drawn and bloodied" in search of Cicero's brother, Quintus, who managed to escape with the help of his slaves and freedmen. Later, they beat the tribune Sestius so badly that he was left for dead.[57]

There is no evidence for any direct involvement by Fulvia in any of this. Rather, she seems to have stayed out of the limelight during her marriage to Clodius, as a proper Roman matron should. She and her mother did, however, play small roles in one episode in the years-long conflict between her husband and Cicero. At issue was the restoration to Cicero of property he owned on the Palatine hill, Rome's most prestigious neighborhood. The house itself had been destroyed by a mob after he fled the city. Clodius later purchased the land, as well as an adjoining plot, for a new home. When Cicero returned from exile, the senate

---

55. Cic., *Att.* 3.4 = *SBA* 49; Plut., *Vit. Cic.* 32.1; Cass. Dio 38.17.6–7. See Kaster 2006, 412–3 and Kelly 2006, 225–37.
56. Tatum 1999, 166–75; Seager 2002, 101–9.
57. Cic., *Sest.* 75–9 with Kaster's commentary (2006, 285–94); Plut., *Vit. Pomp.* 49.3 and *Vit. Cic.* 33.3–4.

ordered the restoration of his property, but Clodius argued that the land could not be returned to Cicero because he (Clodius) had consecrated a temple to the goddess Liberty (Libertas) on part of the property, and it now belonged to her. The crux of the problem was a matter of sacred law: could a space that had been consecrated to a deity be deconsecrated at a later point? The case was to be decided by a jury of priests called *pontifices*, experts in religious law. We do not have the speech that Clodius delivered in court, but Cicero's rebuttal (*De Domo Sua*, "About His Own House") survives.

In the speech, Cicero attacks Clodius's position from several angles, the most significant of which is Cicero's assertion that Liberty's shrine had never been properly consecrated in the first place. In Roman religion, the accurate performance of rituals was paramount: any error in prayer formulae or in ritual action vitiated an entire rite. This is the same logic that demanded that the Vestal Virgins repeat the sacrifice to the Bona Dea after Clodius escaped from Caesar's house. Cicero argued that the consecration of the shrine had been thoroughly bungled by the newly appointed pontifex who performed it. The new priest was Lucius Pinarius Natta, Fulvia's half-brother, who was, Cicero claims, goaded into assisting his brother-in-law Clodius in this farcical ritual by his sister and mother.[58] Fulvia's willingness to draw on family connections suggests a real commitment to her husband's political goals. In the end, however, Cicero got his property back.

Milo

For the rest of Clodius's career, whether he was in office or out, he wielded tremendous power through his popularity with the urban masses that stemmed from the package of legislation he presented during his tribunate. Clodius continued to use his power to pursue his political enemies relentlessly. These included Titus Annius Milo, one of the tribunes in 57 who had worked to bring Cicero back to Rome. Milo enjoyed support from the optimates and from Pompey, who increasingly distanced himself from Caesar, whom he treated as a rival for supremacy rather than

---

58. Cic., *Dom.* 118 and 139. Nisbet (1939, 168) identifies the sister in question as an otherwise unknown Pinaria, but Taylor (1942, 396–7) made the argument, now widely accepted, that Cicero means Fulvia. A good translation of Cicero's speech with useful notes is found in Shackleton Bailey 1991, 37–101.

a close ally. Of Crassus in this period, nothing is known. For his part, Milo ran his own gangs to counter Clodius's. Over the next several years, Clodius and Milo and their supporters would continue to fight over control of the city on the streets and in the courts. The Roman government, which never in the five-hundred-year history of the Republic had maintained a police force in the city, was powerless to stop the violence.

The running conflict between Clodius and Milo came to a head in late 53, a year notable for the fact that the city had become so ungovernable that no consuls were installed in office until July (they usually entered on January 1). This was due in part to the fact that three of the four candidates for that top office had been caught up in a bribery scandal so large that it caused a cash shortage severe enough to double the interest rate at which money was lent in the city.[59] The consuls were inaugurated so late in 53 that it was almost immediately time to hold elections for 52. Yet because the situation remained volatile, this next election, too, was delayed so long that again, when the new year arrived, there were no elected officials to take over control of the city. Among the candidates for office in 52 were Milo, who was campaigning for the consulship, and Clodius, who sought the praetorship.

On January 17, 52, Clodius set out with three traveling companions and a posse of twenty-six armed slaves, a normal-sized security detail for an aristocrat in those dangerous days,[60] for a quick trip to Aricia. Fulvia and the children stayed at the family's new house on the Palatine hill.[61] We are fortunate that the details of what happened the following day, Clodius's last, and in the weeks after that, were hashed out in a trial later in the spring. They are preserved in some narrative accounts and in the text of the closing defense speech Cicero wrote for the occasion. Equally important is the very valuable commentary on that speech written by a scholar named Asconius, who had access to the court records from the trial.[62]

But let us return to our tale. Clodius was to deliver a speech to Aricia's town council later on the 17th, probably in connection with his

---

59. Cic., *Att.* 4.17.2–4 = *SBA* 91.2-4, *QFr.* 2.15.4 = *SBQ* 19.4; App. *BCiv.* 2.19; Cass. Dio 40.45. Appius, Clodius's older brother and consul of 54, was caught up in the scandal but did not suffer for it.

60. Lintott 1968, 83–5.

61. Asc., *Mil.* 31C. This is not the same house whose construction famously embroiled Clodius in a legal contest with Cicero in late 57 (see pp. 39–40).

62. App., *BCiv.* 2.21–4; Cass. Dio 40.47–54. Asconius thought Cicero's speech, *Pro Milone* (On Behalf of Milo), was the orator's best work (Asc., *Mil.* 42C).

current campaign for the praetorship. The traveling party worked its way sixteen miles south from Rome along the Via Appia, the earliest of Rome's major roads, which had been built in 312 BCE by Clodius's ancestor, Appius Claudius Caecus.[63] Some of the details of the next twenty-four hours are hazy, but the rough outline is clear. Having dispatched his duty in Aricia, Clodius either stayed the night there or headed back toward Rome that evening, stopping at his own villa outside the town of Bovillae, which lay about one-third of the way back along the via Appia. Travel in the Roman world was always a dangerous proposition—hence Clodius's bodyguards—and it was doubly unwise to travel after dark. Bandits were everywhere.

Wherever they spent the night, Clodius's party enjoyed part of the next day, January 18, at his villa. They also made a visit to Pompey's house nearby, despite knowing that Pompey was at that time enjoying the seaside pleasures of the Etruscan coast.[64] Meanwhile, that same morning in Rome, Milo attended a public assembly where he was harassed by a tribune loyal to Clodius, and then he went to a meeting of the senate. Having finished his business for the day, Milo headed home to collect his wife and bodyguard (a troop of armed slaves and gladiators) and to change his shoes before starting on a trip to his hometown of Lanuvium, which lay just a few miles past Aricia on the Via Appia. Milo had some official business to attend to there.[65]

At some point in the middle of the afternoon, just outside of Bovillae, Clodius's party and Milo's met on the road, one heading north to Rome and the other heading south to Lanuvium. The two groups passed one another mostly without incident until two gladiators named Eudamus and Birria, who were bringing up the rear of Milo's entourage, began to taunt Clodius's slaves. They responded in kind. Clodius turned to see what was causing the commotion, at which point Birria hurled a spear at him, hitting him in the shoulder. At this point, anger on both sides boiled over and men rushed into the fray. A few carried the wounded Clodius into a nearby tavern. Milo, calculating that a wounded Clodius was more dangerous than a dead one, ordered his men to drag Clodius

---

63. This is the same Appius Claudius, censor in 312, whose two sons founded the main branches of the family (see p. 20). For more on the censor and his road, see K.-L. Elvers, *BNP*, s.v. "Claudius I.2" and M. Rathmann, *BNP*, s.v. "Via Appia."

64. Cic., *Mil.* 54.

65. Cicero reports (*Mil.* 27 and 45) that Milo held the position of *dictator* ("chief magistrate") at Lanuvium, and he argues that because of this Clodius knew Milo would be traveling to town on the 18th of January in order to install a new priest and oversee some public sacrifices.

out of the inn. Clodius was then quickly and brutally dispatched near a shrine of the Bona Dea (Cicero would later imply that this was divine retribution for Clodius's violation of the goddess's ritual a decade before). When the fight was over, there was no one to convey Clodius's body back to Rome—most of his slaves were either dead or severely wounded—so it was left on the road. A passing senator, Sextus Teidius, riding in a litter on his way back to the capital from his own villa, found Clodius's corpse. He ordered his slaves to carry the body to Rome in the litter, while the senator himself walked back to his country estate. Teidius was no fool: the powder keg that was Rome was going to explode.

News of Clodius's death reached Rome before his body arrived. Fulvia is sometimes blamed for the events that happened that night and the next day, but while she certainly played a role, it is clear from the sources that other of Clodius's allies were involved and that, ultimately, no one could control the mob of his supporters.[66] The crowd met his corpse at his home on the Palatine. Fulvia wept before them. Her enemies later accused her of putting on a show to whip up the crowd. Such a charge entirely discounts the possibility of genuine grief on Fulvia's part, but it probably stems in part from the fact that Fulvia did not follow proper protocol for an aristocratic funeral. Her actions fanned the flames of the mob's anger toward Milo.[67] Rather than keeping the crowd away until she could display Clodius's body properly—that is, cleansed, dressed in a toga, surrounded by the insignia of his highest office, and carefully laid out in the front hall of their home—Fulvia allowed people to view Clodius immediately: unwashed, bloodied, and exposed, his many wounds clearly visible.

By the next morning, the crowd had grown, and some of Clodius's more prominent allies arrived at the house. Among them were two tribunes who persuaded the crowd to bring the naked, wounded corpse down the hill to the Forum and display it on the rostra, the speakers' podium that sat in front of the senate house. Fulvia, who as the female head of house would normally have been in charge of funeral arrangements, must have given her consent.[68]

---

66. See, for example, Sumi 1997.

67. Fulvia's weeping: Asc., *Mil.* 32C; Harders 2019, 122. Gladhill 2018 offers an excellent reconstruction of Fulvia's role in the immediate aftermath of Clodius's death and at Milo's trial. In the following, I follow his reading of the inverted funeral.

68. See Šterbenc Erker 2011, esp. 47–8 on the gendered division of labor in Roman funerals. Sumi argues (1997, 95) that Fulvia had ample time to prepare a proper funeral, and the fact that she did not do so reveals her plan to continue to manipulate the crowd by displaying Clodius's body in the Forum. This grossly underestimates the amount of preparation required for the elaborate

Everything that followed this decision was a perversion of a normal aristocratic funeral. It was standard procedure for the body of a deceased politician to be escorted from his home to the Forum, where laudatory speeches would be delivered as the body was displayed on the rostra. The escort normally comprised family members, friends and dependents, and, most impressively, a group of actors who played the part of the man's most distinguished male ancestors, wearing both the insignia of each relative's highest office and his death mask.[69] As a Claudius Pulcher by birth, Clodius's funeral should have included a spectacular number of these, along with his two brothers dressed in their magisterial regalia. It would have been a vivid reminder of the Claudian clan's prestige, dignity, and service to the state. Instead, Clodius's funeral cortege was rather less dignified and much angrier.

In place of the normal eulogy recounting Clodius's most important achievements, the tribunes delivered harangues to the crowd, pointing to Clodius's gaping, unwashed wounds. They incited their audience until it could no longer be restrained. Turning to the senate house, the crowd rushed in to heap up benches, platforms, tables, and copyists' notebooks. They placed Clodius's body on top of the pile and set it alight, an impromptu funeral pyre right in the heart of Rome, rather than the carefully constructed pyre that should have received the body outside the walls of the city. The flames quickly jumped to the building, burning it down to the ground, along with another government building next door. Rioters then attacked Milo's house, only to be driven off by a barrage of arrows.

The worst of their resentment spent, the crowd cast about for someone to take charge of the situation. Some went to the grove of the goddess Libitina, where funeral paraphernalia was kept, including mock (?) magisterial insignia that were used by the actors who were hired for funeral processions. The insignia included *fasces*, bundles of wooden rods that signaled the power of a man's office.[70] The mob carried the *fasces* from the shrine first to the homes of two of Milo's rivals for the consulship. Neither

spectacle that was an aristocratic Roman funeral. Clodius's body arrived in Rome in the early evening and was moved to the Forum the next morning. Sumi's imagined time frame hardly leaves time to recover from the shock of the murder, let alone hiring an undertaker, arranging hired mourners and actors for the funeral procession, ordering construction of a funeral pyre, and writing of eulogy. There will barely have been enough time to alert family and friends and to try to discover exactly what had transpired.

69. The most famous description of this practice is found in Polyb. 6.53–4.
70. Sumi 1997, 100–2.

man was willing to take them up. Then the crowd moved on to Pompey's house and implored him to take control of the city.

The Trial

The situation was so volatile that emergency measures were necessary. Recognizing that things were out of their control and that they needed Pompey's help, the senate issued a *senatus consultum ultimum* ("Final Decree") that gave Pompey, the tribunes, and the *interrex* (an official who had finally been selected to hold the long delayed elections) the power to do "whatever was necessary to preserve the state."[71] Some began to say that Pompey should be named dictator, an office only filled in times of crisis. In order to avoid giving Pompey the unlimited power that came with that title, however, senatorial conservatives compromised, allowing Pompey to be appointed sole consul. This was a double novelty. Never before had a consul been simply chosen by the senate (rather than elected by the people), nor had one ever been seated in that office without a colleague.[72]

Since many in the city seem to have been more disturbed by the burning of the senate house than by the death of Clodius, and since Milo still had many powerful supporters (including Cicero, Cato, the leading conservative, and Caelius, the man who had been accused of trying to poison Clodia), Milo thought it was safe to return to the city. He snuck back into Rome the night after the conflagration at the senate house. His allies put out the word that Clodius had set an ambush for Milo and that Milo had only acted in self-defense. Milo's enemies offered as a counter-narrative that Milo had laid the ambush for Clodius. The dead man's nephews, both named Appius Claudius, prepared to prosecute Milo for Clodius's murder. Clodius's friend Antonius signed on to assist them.[73] Pompey, who had supported Milo as a counter-weight to

---

71. In the last century of the Republic, as the state faced crisis after crisis, the Romans had increasing recourse to the Final Decree, also called an *s.c.u.* It was a tool of dubious legality, and the men who enforced it often paid a penalty for doing so. The most famous of these was Cicero who, despite having been given an *s.c.u.* and having the backing of the senate, was exiled by Clodius (see p. 38) for executing citizens without a trial. For a concise discussion, see Lintott 1999, 89–93.

72. Some months later, when the worst of the crisis had passed, Pompey appointed his father-in-law as his colleague. Plut., *Vit. Pomp.* 54–5; Cass. Dio 40.51.1–52.3; App., *BCiv.* 2.22–5.

73. Asc., *Mil.* 33C–34C; Cic., *Mil.* 70; App., *BCiv.* 2.22–3. The Appii were biological brothers, the two sons of Clodius's middle brother, Gaius Claudius Pulcher. The elder son was, following custom,

Clodius, now saw an opportunity to remove Milo as a candidate for the consulship: Pompey preferred other men for the top job. He withdrew his support from Milo, letting it be known that he feared Milo would try to assassinate him. Even so, Cicero, Cato, and a host of other prominent conservatives signed on for Milo's defense at the trial, set to begin in early April.

Milo's opponents kept the matter before the public in the ensuing months. Tribunes of the plebs who were allied with Clodius called a series of public meetings, where their speeches whipped the crowd into frenzied anger against Milo and Cicero, his main defender. Similar efforts were underway in the senate, too. In a speech there a few weeks after the clash on the via Appia, another of Clodius's allies gave an exaggerated account of what had occurred on January 18,[74] saying that it was Milo who had intended to ambush Clodius, not the other way around. He claimed that Milo had left Rome with an entourage of 300 armed men, a force that easily overwhelmed Clodius's handful of slaves, and that after the murder, Milo had gone to Clodius's villa looking to kill Clodius's young son, who was rumored to be hiding there. Upon discovering that the boy was not at the house, Milo cut one of Clodius's slaves limb from limb and slit the throats of some others. Whether or not any of this was true mattered very little.

Fulvia, too, was a powerful reminder of the public's loss. Simply by fulfilling the normal obligations that came with widowhood, she made it impossible to forget what had happened. For a period of ten months after Clodius's death, she appeared in public in appropriate mourning attire: dark clothing, including a cloak and possibly a special head covering. She was expected to eschew makeup and jewelry.[75] Every time she left the house, everyone would be reminded of her grief. The house itself prevented people from forgetting as well. If scholars have correctly identified the location of their home on the Palatine hill, it was visible from the Forum, which sat at the base of the hill. Everyone going about his business there, the political heart of the city, would have been able

---

named Gaius after his father. The younger son, also following custom, was named for his grandfather, Appius. The older of these two, Gaius, was at some point adopted by his father's brother, Appius Claudius, the consul of 54, at which time he took on the name of his adoptive father. Thus both biological brothers, adoptive cousins, came to be named Appius Claudius Pulcher. Antonius's assistance with the case against Milo is recorded by Asconius (*Mil.* 41C).

74. Asc., *Mil.* 34C–35C.
75. Olson 2008, 41–2.

to look up and see the cut cypress trees that Fulvia, following Roman custom, would have set in front of the house to advertise that the family was in mourning.[76]

Efforts to keep the story a live issue were successful. Rome had not calmed down very much by the time Milo's trial began in early April. Trials in Rome were often held out in the open, and crowds would gather to watch. Usually this was just for entertainment, but not this time. The audience's mood was so volatile and there was so much public anger directed at Milo that, at the end of the first day of the proceedings, the presiding magistrate had to request from Pompey an armed guard to keep the peace as the case moved forward.

The prosecution took an unusual, but highly effective, approach for closing their case. They concluded their witness list with a series of women whose testimony packed a punch. First, a group of priestesses of Vesta from Bovillae[77] testified that an unknown woman had come to them at the behest of Milo to fulfill a vow he had made for Clodius's death. These were followed by tearful testimonies from Sempronia and Fulvia. Asconius, who was able to read summaries of their testimony (or perhaps even verbatim accounts) in the court records, does not preserve their words. He does, however, attest to the powerful effect their tears had on the jury and the larger audience.[78]

In the late afternoon, after the prosecution had laid out its case and court had adjourned for the day, a tribune of the plebs delivered a rousing speech to the crowd that had hung around the Forum. He urged them to attend court the next day to hear the closing arguments of the defense, to make their opinions known to the jury, and not to allow Milo to escape. The next morning, Pompey took steps to control the scene by ordering shops closed for the day and deploying troops in the Forum and along the thoroughfares leading to it. Cicero spoke for the defense, arguing that all the evidence pointed toward an act of self-defense by

---

76. Gladhill 2018, 301–2.
77. Asconius identifies them as "Alban Virgins" (*Mil.* 40C). The Romans believed that the cult of Vesta at Alba Longa predated the founding of Rome (Livy 1.3.11): the mother of Romulus and Remus was reported to have been made a Vestal Virgin there in order to prevent her from having a son who might challenge her uncle's usurpation of the throne. Although some have made the case that the women who appeared at Milo's trial were priestesses of the Bona Dea (e.g., Lewis 2006, 246), an inscription from Rome makes clear they belonged to Vesta (*CIL* 6.2172 = *AE* 2001.169 and 2006.19). That the cult was transferred at some point to the nearby town of Bovillae is suggested by another inscription in a dedication by a local official of Bovillae whose sister was an Alban Virgin (*CIL* 14.2410 = *AE* 2006.270, from Marino).
78. Gladhill 2018.

Milo. He was heckled so badly by the crowd that he could not speak with his usual polish. In the end, the crowd got what it wanted: Milo was convicted and sent into exile in the city of Massilia on the southern coast of Gaul (modern Marseilles in France). Sometime later, Cicero sent him a copy of the speech that he had planned to deliver; this is what survives today. Milo famously responded he was glad that Cicero had not been able to give that version of the speech in court that day. If he had, Milo would not then be enjoying the delectable seafood Massilia had to offer.[79]

The conviction of Milo drew this chapter of Fulvia's life to a close. Leaving girlhood behind, upon her marriage she had become a Roman matron, the head of a prominent aristocratic household, a mother of two, and a valuable political asset to her husband. Although she was not born into a politically active household, Fulvia had clearly learned vital lessons about managing public perception during her time in her stepfather's home and the decade she spent married to one of Rome's most unpredictable and aggressive politicians. She demonstrated her commitment to Clodius's political aims by helping to persuade her half-brother to help Clodius consecrate Liberty's shrine. Furthermore, the decisions she made in the hours after Clodius's death demonstrated real political acumen and fortitude. She not only helped stoke public hostility toward her husband's killer, but eventually faced him in court. She delivered effective testimony, swaying a jury in a setting that so unnerved the polished and experienced Cicero that his oratory was rendered impotent. When we first see Fulvia in public, she is already a force with which to reckon.

---

79. Cass. Dio 40.54.

3

Life with Curio and Antonius

By the middle of November 52, Fulvia was free to put aside her mourning attire. Although Roman society revered women who remained loyal to the memory of their deceased husbands, it was fairly common for widows, especially young ones, to remarry, and many did so shortly after the required ten months of mourning had ended. For example, Cicero's daughter, Tullia, was widowed in 57 at the age of 20 and remarried the next year; Cornelia married Pompey in 52, just a year after her husband, the son of Crassus, had died alongside his father at the battle of Carrhae. The exact timing of Fulvia's second marriage—to Gaius Scribonius Curio, son of the consul of 76 and, in his own right, a rising force in politics in the late 50s—cannot be recovered, but it appears to have happened in late 52 or early in 51. Had the marriage happened too soon, it would have been a scandal that Cicero could never have allowed to pass unremarked. Beyond honoring a general sense of propriety, the ten-month mourning period ensured that there would never be any question about the paternity of a man's posthumous offspring.[1]

It is worth pausing at this point to highlight one of the things that our sources generally do *not* say about Fulvia. Despite the overwhelmingly negative portrait of her painted by ancient sources, she is almost never accused of sexual impropriety.[2] As far as the ancient tradition is concerned, Fulvia's main characteristics are greed and aggression, not lasciviousness. This is rather surprising because such claims were part

---

1. Gardner 1986, 50–4.
2. Cicero's rather tame accusation that Antonius had an affair with Fulvia while she was still married to Clodius will be dealt with later in this chapter. The other important locus for sexual allegations against Fulvia is Octavian's epigram, discussed in the next chapter, that paints her as extraordinarily aggressive.

Fulvia. Celia E. Schultz, Oxford University Press. © Oxford University Press 2021.
DOI: 10.1093/oso/9780190697136.003.0003

and parcel of Roman invective, frequently used against both male and female targets. We have already seen Cicero deploy this particular weapon against both Clodius and his sister, Clodia Metelli, whom Cicero accused of incest with one another. He further accused Clodius of submitting to the desires of the pirates who kidnapped him in the early 60s,[3] and he implied frequent debaucheries when he claimed that Clodius traveled with an entourage of effeminate Greeks and prostitutes. And as we will see, he launched similar attacks on Fulvia's second and third husbands. Cicero attacked Clodia mercilessly in his defense speech for his friend, Caelius, whom Clodia had accused in court of attempting to poison her. He hammered home to his audience that Clodia's widowhood had left her free to operate like a common courtesan.[4] Set in the context of the invective leveled against Fulvia's closest associates, the lack of a similar tradition about Fulvia strongly suggests that her behavior on this account was (nearly) irreproachable.

A Second Marriage

After Clodius's death, Fulvia was in a relatively secure position: bereft, but not destitute. Her dowry will have been returned to her, and she is likely to have been left a share of Clodius's property. Even if he had not made a will, or if he had left the entirety of his property to his children, it was not unusual in Fulvia's day for widows to continue to enjoy the benefits and income from estates that would ultimately come into the possession of their children.[5] When Fulvia chose to re-enter the marriage market—and indeed as a mature woman, this will have been more her own decision than it was when she was a teenager—she did so from a much stronger position than she had when she first caught Clodius's eye. In addition to her other attractions—wealth, demonstrated fertility, and matronal propriety—Fulvia was now an even more valuable political asset than she had been before.[6] It was nothing new for a Roman politician to advertise his allegiance to a particular sector of the population

---

3. Cic., *Har. resp.* 42. For a similar accusation against Fulvia's third husband, Antonius, see Cic., *Phil.* 2.44–5.
4. For example, Cic., *Cael.* 49.
5. On the rules regarding the return of a woman's dowry, see Treggiari 1991, 350–64 and 498–501; Gardner 1986, 107.
6. Welch 1995, 186–7.

through his female attachments; the man who married Fulvia would be well positioned to present himself as the heir to Clodius's considerable political power. For example, some years before, Caesar had advertised himself as a champion of the people and an opponent of Sulla by refusing the dictator's demand that he divorce his then-wife, Cornelia, a daughter of Sulla's political opponent, Cinna. To this same end, Caesar proudly discussed his aunt Julia's marriage to Marius, Sulla's primary political rival, at her funeral in 69.[7]

We know nothing about Fulvia's life with Curio. In fact, the marriage itself is attested only once, and in a very roundabout way. Our source is, once again, Cicero. In one of the devastating speeches he delivered against Antonius in the aftermath of Caesar's death, Cicero taunted Antonius, saying that his house contained the same deadly thing that proved fatal for Clodius and Curio. This is not much to work with. We do know, however, that the marriage produced one son (also named Gaius Scribonius Curio) whose existence is also attested by a single reference—to his death.[8]

If Fulvia did not already know Curio when she was a young, unmarried girl, she is likely to have met him through Clodius and his brothers: they moved in the same social circles, and Curio's family had been staunch supporters of Clodius in his time of greatest need. Curio's father defended him in the Bona Dea trial, and Curio himself was mockingly identified by Cicero as the leader of the *barbatuli iuvenes*, "young men with budding beards," that is, the fashionable sons of senatorial and equestrian families who rallied around Clodius at the time of the scandal.[9] Both Clodius and Curio had been, in their youth, friends with Antonius, who would eventually become Fulvia's third husband. Clodius's ties to Antonius were not especially strong, and indeed they had a rather famous falling out in 53 over an unspecified issue (on which, see p. 71). Curio and Antonius, however, had been very close. They shared a reputation for indulging in wine and women—and each other: years after Curio's death, Cicero alleged in a meeting of the senate that Curio and Antonius had been lovers. Further evidence of their louche lifestyle was the enormous debts the two young men racked up.[10]

---

7. Plut., *Vit. Caes.* 1.1 and 5.2.
8. Marriage: Cic., *Phil.* 2.11. Son: Cass. Dio, 51.2.5.
9. Cic., *Att.* 1.14.5 and 1.16.11 = *SBA* 14.5 and 16.11.
10. Cic., *Phil.* 2.44–6; Plut., *Vit. Ant.* 2.3–4 and *Vit. Pomp.* 58.1.

Curio's pedigree was much less prestigious than Clodius's. Curio was born in 84 (thus he was a few years older than Fulvia) to parents descended from plebeian nobility. His mother, Memmia, came from a family that had long been active in politics. Curio's father's family, however, had only reached the height of polite society at Rome a few years after Curio's birth, with Curio senior's consulship in 76.[11] Throughout the 50s, the politics of both Curio senior and junior were generally conservative and distinctly independent. They rarely allowed their personal relationships with other politicians to drive their decision-making on important issues. A good example is the fact that father and son worked at cross-purposes to Clodius when they advocated for Cicero's return from exile in 57, even though the senior Curio had earlier defended, and his son had publicly supported, Clodius in the Bona Dea scandal a few years before. Likewise, in the summer of 53, Cicero felt he could ask the younger Curio to throw his support behind the candidacy of Clodius's nemesis, Milo, for the consulship of 52.[12] We do not know what Curio's answer was, but it is unlikely that Cicero would have asked if rejection were a foregone conclusion.

Throughout most of his career, the younger Curio was an outspoken defender of senatorial authority, and he had been a vigorous opponent of the alliance of Caesar, Pompey, and Crassus from its earliest formation. In the decade that followed, as his colleagues one by one took sides in the escalating dispute between Pompey and Caesar—which passed the point of no return in 53 with the death of Crassus—Curio continued his opposition to them both. It was only when civil war was imminent that Curio finally threw in his lot with Caesar.[13]

Curio's contemporaries—Caesar, Cicero, and Caelius (Clodia's former lover)—seem to have both appreciated Curio's finer qualities and been aware of his foibles. In letters to Cicero, who was out of Rome serving as governor of the province of Cilicia in what is now Turkey, Caelius warmly refers to him as *Curio noster* ("our friend Curio") but describes him as impulsive and fickle.[14] Cicero's attitude was equally mixed. In the same letter to Atticus in which he describes the *barbatuli*

---

11. On the senior Curio, see McDermott 1972 and Tatum 1991. For Curio's mother, see Sisenna F31 = *FRHist.* 2.624.

12. Cic., *Fam.* 2.6.1–5 = *SBF* 50.1–5.

13. The idea that Fulvia was behind Curio's change of heart (Babcock 1965, 9; Fischer 1999, 23–5 and 62) is not supported by the ancient sources.

14. Cic., *Fam.* 8.6.5 and 8.14.4 = *SBF* 88.5 and 97.4.

iuvenes, Cicero disparagingly refers to the young man as *duce filiola Curionis* ("the ringleader, Curio's little daughter"), and he implies in another letter that Curio was known for shooting off his mouth: "You know the man. He kept nothing secret."[15] Despite all this, and despite Curio's friendship with some of Cicero's least favorite people (Clodius and Antonius foremost among them), Curio and Cicero maintained a friendship that is attested by several letters and by references in other letters that Cicero wrote to his friend Atticus.[16] Even as Cicero and Curio were on different sides in the civil war between Caesar and Pompey, the two could still spend an overnight visit talking over the course of the conflict.[17] Later, after Curio's death, Cicero would write that his young friend had been a skilled orator who would have achieved the heights of power, if only he had sought better counsel.[18] Caesar, whose cause Curio took up on the eve of war with Pompey (on which, more later), gives Curio a prominent role in his account of the conflict, presenting Curio as very much the same man Caelius and Cicero knew: hotheaded, overconfident, yet also fiercely loyal.[19]

In terms of his personality, Curio seems to have been cut from the same cloth as Clodius, and history has assessed them similarly: decadent, dangerous, and skilled politicians out to destroy the system that promoted them. Curio's reputation suffered badly in the decades after the fall of the Republic: he came to be seen as a corrupt traitor. The historian Velleius Paterculus, writing almost seventy-five years after Curio's death, describes him as "a man of noble birth, eloquent, rash, reckless with his money and his chastity—and with everyone else's, wickedly clever, and a powerful speaker to the detriment of the state. No amount of money, no pleasures were able to satisfy him." The poet Lucan, writing another thirty years after Velleius, speaks of "reckless Curio, with his corruptible tongue." The imperial biographer Suetonius called Curio the most violent of the tribunes.[20] Like many of his contemporaries, Curio was not above using gang violence to achieve his political goals, and he

---

15. Cic., *Att.* 10.4.8 = SBA 195.8. Cf. Cic., *Att.* 2.12.2 = SBA 30.2.
16. Letters to Curio: Cic., *Fam.* 2.1–7 = SBF 45–50 and 107. Warm references to Curio are also found in *Att.* 2.12.2, 6.2.6, and 6.3.4 = SBA 30.2, 116.6, and 117.4.
17. Cic., *Att.* 10.4.6–11 and 10.5.2 = SBA 195.6–11 and 196.2.
18. *Brut.* 280–1.
19. The main narrative of Curio's service in the Civil War is Caes., *B Civ.* 2.23–42. See also Cass. Dio 51.41.1–42.7 and App., *B. Civ.* 2.44–5. On Caesar's Curio as "an apt spokesperson for loyalty," see Batstone and Damon 2006, 98–101.
20. Vell. Pat. 2.48.3; Luc. 1.269; Suet., *Iul.* 29.1. On *audax* as a key term in Roman political invective, see Wirszubski 1961.

is reported to have physically attacked an opponent—Clodius's oldest brother, Appius—in a meeting of the senate at which Appius sought to remove Curio from the list of senators.[21] Since most of this same profile fit not only Clodius but also Fulvia's third husband, Antonius, one could be forgiven for wondering if Fulvia had a preferred type.

Curio's Career

Regardless of when they first met, Fulvia and Curio probably became reacquainted at about the time she became a widow. Late in 53 or, more likely, early in 52, Curio returned to the capital after a stint in the province of Asia on the staff of the governor, who happened to be Clodius's middle brother, Gaius. The exact nature of Curio's position is not recorded in the sources, but he was probably there as a quaestor, making this position his first elected office.[22] We do not know how he spent his first few months back in Rome, including what role, if any, he played in the political chaos that dominated the city for the first half of 52 (Clodius's death, Milo's trial, and Pompey's sole consulship). Seeking political office was probably already on his mind—it certainly was on the minds of his supporters. Several of the surviving letters that Cicero wrote to Curio while the younger man was still in Asia stress how positive were the reports of his conduct, how eager people were to see him back in the capital, and how high were expectations for his political future. For whatever reason, Curio decided not to campaign right away. Perhaps the dangerously unstable situation in the city made it seem wise to hang back.

Even so, Curio did take some steps to increase his visibility. The most important step he took was to marry Fulvia, thus positioning himself to draw support from the same groups that had supported Clodius: the urban poor and the powerful senatorial clique around his brothers.[23] The most flamboyant step Curio took was the celebration of his father's funeral games. The old man had died while Curio was abroad, and there

---

21. Cic., *Phil.* 2.4; Cass. Dio 40.63.5–64.2.
22. Holding the quaestorship guaranteed a man entry to the senate (Lintott 1999, 136), and Curio is certainly a member of the senate in October 51 (Cic., *Fam.* 8.8.5 = *SBF* 84.5), before he held his only securely attested office, the tribunate of 50. Lacey (1961, 320) is more certain of the quaestorship than Broughton, *MRR* 2.224, s.a. 54. Recovering the details of Curio's actions from late 53 until his election in 51 is very difficult. See Linderski 1972 for a careful analysis.
23. Tatum 1999, 69–71.

had been some debate about whether the games should be arranged in his name while he was still out of town or if the matter should be deferred until his return.[24] In the end, Curio put on a memorable display, possibly in 52 but more likely in the summer of 51, just as he was preparing to run for office,[25] when the games would have had their greatest value as an advertisement for Curio's campaign. It appears that he was originally planning to run for the aedileship that year, but he must have withdrawn from that competition when a spot unexpectedly opened up on the college of tribunes of the plebs: one of the newly elected tribunes was prevented from taking office by being convicted in court (the nature of the crime is unclear) after the election.[26] Curio successfully campaigned to replace him.

Funeral games were a festive celebration that honored the memory of a prominent Roman. Organized by his heirs at some point after the funeral, the games usually lasted several days and were attended by family, friends, and members of the public. While technically a private affair, by Curio's day they had long been used by ambitious men to curry favor with voters as they advertised themselves as public benefactors. Gifts and food were sometimes distributed, and the entertainments usually included gladiatorial competitions and theatrical performances. Funeral games were a prime venue for aristocratic competition: one always wanted to exceed what came before.

The games that Curio organized for his father were not remarkable for the quality or the type of entertainments they offered. Curio seems to have planned fairly standard fare, with theatrical performances, athletic competitions (probably boxers and wrestlers), and an animal hunt involving exotic panthers.[27] Nor were the games known for their

24. Cic., *Fam.* 2.2–3 = *SBF* 46 and 47.
25. Scholars disagree on the date of the games, but most assume that Curio held them shortly after he returned from the east or in the following year. The consensus opinion, however, overlooks a reference to Curio's theater in a letter from Caelius to Cicero that is dated to June 51 (Cic., *Fam.* 8.2.1 = *SBF* 78.1) and a second report, from September of that same year, that Curio had given panthers he had used in his games to Caelius for use in his (*Fam.* 8.9.3 = *SBF* 82.3). Wooden theaters like Curio's were intended to be temporary structures, taken down after the event or, at most, after the season (cf. Tac., *Ann.* 14.21). They were not well constructed and occasionally collapsed with disastrous effects (e.g., Tac., *Ann.* 4.62 and Suet., *Tib.* 40), an indication that Curio's construction was unlikely to have survived the winter of 52–51 and still been in use later that summer. On wooden theaters, see Sear 2006, 55–7. On Rome's late adoption of stone theaters, see Manuwald 2011, 55–68.
26. Cic., *Fam.* 8.4.2 = *SBF* 81.2.
27. The panthers, or at least some of them, survived unharmed. Curio was able to hand them off to Caelius, who needed some wild animals for the games he was hosting as part of his official duties as aedile (Cic., *Fam.* 8.9.3 = *SBF* 82.3). On beast hunts as popular entertainment at Rome, see Epplett 2014. Athletes: Plin., *Nat.* 36.24.120 with Lee 2014, 535–6.

lavishness: Curio was not particularly wealthy by the standards of Rome's highest social class, and in 51 he is said to have been rebuffed by Caesar when he requested a loan (to pay for the games?).[28] What was remarkable about the celebration in honor of Curio's father was its venue. Curio arranged for the construction of not one, but two wooden theaters. Temporary theaters like these, built for specific events, were common in Rome at the time. The city had just been endowed with its first permanent, stone theater in Pompey's Temple of Venus Victrix, but wooden theaters continued to be used for private events and smaller celebrations for centuries afterward.[29] What caused a stir about Curio's theaters was partly that there were two of them, but mostly it was that the two theaters, each in the shape of a semi-circle, were set on revolving pivots.[30] This allowed them to be swung away from one another so that two different plays could be put on at the same time, or they could be swung around in the other direction so that they could form a complete ring of stadium seating for the viewing of gladiatorial competitions or animal hunts. Curio had created Rome's first documented amphitheater.

The design was so scandalous that the elder Pliny, writing more than a century later, twice describes Curio's extravagance as madness (*insania, furor*). Pliny alleges that Curio had taken an already dangerous structure (wooden theaters were known to collapse periodically, killing audience members) and made it even more so. Pliny is horrified that members of the public willingly sat in the structure, even when the theaters were being swung on their pivots. Pliny put the potential disaster of their collapse on a par with Rome's greatest military disaster, the loss at the battle of Cannae in the Second Carthaginian War:[31]

> For what should one marvel at first? The inventor or the invention? The man who built it or the man who commissioned it? That someone dared to think it up or that someone made it or ordered it? Most astonishing of all is the madness of the populace that dared to sit in so unreliable and

---

28. For Curio's straitened circumstances, see Plin. *HN* 36.116–17 and 120. Loan from Caesar: Cic., *Fam.* 8.4.2 = *SBF* 81.2.

29. See note 25.

30. Davies 2017, 264–5, offers a hypothetical reconstruction of the theater.

31. Plin., *HN* 36.118–20, with Schultze 2007. Pliny's comparison of the theater with Cannae might not be so hyperbolic as it first appears. Livy (22.49.14) says that more than 48,000 Roman soldiers and cavalry died at Cannae. When a theater collapsed at the Italian city of Fidenae in 27 CE, Suetonius claims that 20,000 died (*Tib.* 40). Tacitus (*Ann.* 4.62) puts the number at 50,000.

unstable a seat. Behold! Here is that people—the subduer of the world, the conqueror of the whole globe, who sorts out clans and kingdoms, who gives laws to foreign peoples, a portion, as it were, of the immortal gods here for the benefit of human kind—swaying on a contraption and applauding its own danger! How worthless are our lives! How can we complain about Cannae? What evil could have happened! People grieve when cities are swallowed up by the earth, but behold! Here is the whole of the Roman people, balanced on twin pivots, as if set on two ships! The crowd sees itself struggling, about to die at any moment if the structure is wrenched out of place. And the whole point of this is to garner good will for his future speeches as a tribune, so that he can sway undecided voters! What did he not dare to do on the speakers' podium in front of those whom he persuaded to take part in this!

Hysterics aside, Pliny's depiction of Curio's risk-taking, crowd-pleasing behavior is right in line with how other sources portray him.

Civil War Looms

Curio's long track record of conservative political independence in the senate is often overshadowed, for both ancient writers and modern scholars, by his rather dramatic about-face during his tribunate.[32] When Curio and the other new tribunes took up their office in mid-December of 51, the whole city was anxiously looking forward to March 1 in the coming year, on which date the senate would be free to debate the assignment of provincial commands. This was a pressing matter for Caesar because the outcome, should he be forced to relinquish control of Gaul, had the potential to frustrate his desire to obtain two things he greatly desired—a triumph for his achievements in Gaul and the consulship in 49. Failure to obtain another political office would leave him open to prosecution in court by his enemies.[33]

---

32. On Curio's independence from Caesar and Pompey, see Logghe 2016.

33. Caesar is explicit that, for him, the crux of the matter was that his political enemies had moved against both him and the express will of the people by refusing to allow him to exercise the right they had granted to him run for office without being present in the city (Caes,. *B. Civ.* 1.7–11). Should Caesar relinquish his govenorship and return to private life to run for office, he would also

In the first weeks of his tribunate, Curio seems to have been relatively inactive. Caelius reported to Cicero that things had been moving at a glacial pace until February of 50,[34] when Curio put forward legislation that made clear he wanted to appeal to urban voters who had not too long before been loyal to Clodius: a bill ordering the distribution of gain to the poor and another relating to the roads, the details of which are impossible to recover. On the issue of provincial commands, Curio seems to have worked hard to avoid the showdown between Pompey and Caesar that everyone could see was coming. An early effort to delay the March 1st debate by a few weeks failed, so once debate began, Curio advocated that the two commanders be treated equally, and pushed for an agreement that would remove both Pompey and Caesar from their provincial commands at the same moment. Curio was not in the camp of either general. But by the end of his year in office, Curio was no longer a neutral party. The final straw came on December 1, 50 BCE, when the consul who was presiding over a vote on Curio's most recent proposal summarily dismissed the senate when he saw that Curio's motion to require both Pompey and Caesar lay down their arms had carried, with 370 in favor and only 22 opposed. Cato and the other hard-core conservatives were the holdouts. By dismissing the senate, the consul invalidated the vote. The man then hastened to Pompey's house, where he offered him command of the Republic's forces.[35]

Curio's frustration at his repeated failure to avoid armed conflict was too much to bear, and the city, now under Pompey's control, was no longer safe for him. Straightaway after the vote, he headed north to Gaul. Caesar probably looked like the more reasonable of the two dynasts since he had, on his own, proposed earlier in the summer the same thing that Curio had advocated: that both Caesar and Pompey relinquish their positions and return to private life.[36] Curio's departure from Rome, more than anything else he did, labeled him a traitor to the republican cause, of which Pompey had declared himself the defender.

---

give up leverage to force the senate to grant him the triumph he wanted. The extent to which Caesar was genuinely concerned about Cato's repeated threats to bring him up on charges stemming from his actions in Gaul is much debated. Recently, Morstein-Marx (2007, 2009) has offered a strong argument against the threat of prosecution, but others maintain the concern was real (Ramsey 2009, 48; Morrell 2015, 80).

34. Cic., *Fam.* 8.6.4–5 = *SBF* 88.4–5.
35. App., *B Civ.* 2.30. Cass. Dio 40.63–4 offers a much more hostile portrait of Curio.
36. On Caesar's August proposal: Cic., *Fam.* 8.14.2 = *SBF* 97.2.

Rumors circulated that Curio's allegiance to the Republic had been undercut by a bribe from Caesar.[37]

By January 1, 49, when the new consuls took office, Curio was back in Rome to deliver a letter from Caesar to the Senate. In it, Caesar repeated his earlier offer to lay down arms if Pompey would, too, and threatened war if the offer was not accepted. The new tribunes for 49, including Curio's old friend Antonius, attended an emergency meeting of senate, held on January 7, and they advocated that the senate should accept Caesar's proposal. Many senators remained hostile, and the consuls threw the tribunes out of the meeting. Curio, Antonius, and two other tribunes headed straight to Caesar's camp. Now there was no turning back.

Three days after that fateful meeting of the senate, Caesar crossed the Rubicon. This amounted to an invasion of Italy. Word that he was marching swiftly to Rome caused widespread panic. When he arrived in the capital, he met no armed opposition. The place was a ghost town. Pompey and about half of the Senate had abandoned the capital, at first withdrawing to areas just south of Rome, but ultimately heading to the east where provinces and client kings long loyal to Pompey could offer men and money. Some senators, fearing Caesar's anger, took their families with them when they fled. For other men who were not sure which side to take in the imminent conflict, the decision was less clear. Some stayed in the city, waiting to see what happened. Others left, but did not follow Pompey to Greece. Cicero, who would dither for weeks about what to do, fled the city with his son, brother, and nephew before Caesar's arrival. This was mostly to avoid looking like they supported Caesar rather than to assist Pompey.

We do not know for certain where Fulvia was in all of this, but we can get a sense of the sort of issues she faced by looking at the women of Cicero's family, whose whereabouts are better documented. Cicero's wife, Terentia, and his daughter, Tullia, opted to stay in Rome when their menfolk fled. Cicero worried that this was the wrong decision: he had long maintained his friendship with Caesar, but his adherence to the conservative cause, however reluctant, made it dangerous for members of his family to stay in the city. Yet there were other considerations: Tullia was in the early stages of pregnancy and travel was risky. Also, Terentia and Tullia could be protected by Tullia's husband,

---

37. App., *B Civ.* 2.26–7; Cass. Dio, 40.60–1; Plut., *Caes.* 29–31 and *Pomp.* 58; Lacey 1961.

Dolabella, a loyal Caesarian.[38] The household's situation in early 49 illustrates how the war split families into different political camps and how divided family loyalties could prove beneficial. For those women like Tullia and Fulvia, whose husbands were, at least for the moment, on the right side of things, Rome was a safe place to be. It is therefore likely that Fulvia stayed in the city with her children: Claudia, her older brother, and perhaps already the infant Curio. Fulvia would have been able to look after the family property and to protect Curio's interests while he was out of town, just as Terentia would do for Cicero. If things got too tense, she could withdraw to country estates of her own or other villas belonging to family and friends.

If Fulvia was in Rome in January of 49, she saw the city occupied by Roman soldiers. Before prosecuting his war against Pompey, Caesar took time to improve his political and military position by forcibly taking control of the public treasury in Rome and putting his allies into powerful positions in the city and in the few provinces he controlled. Two of his closest associates were to take charge of affairs in Italy. Marcus Aemilius Lepidus would manage the city of Rome, and Marcus Antonius would hold the whole of Italy.

Curio, too, was given an assignment that reflected Caesar's trust in him. Unlike the earlier round of civil war between the generals Marius and Sulla that had devastated Italy, it was clear that this new conflict would be fought on multiple fronts throughout the empire. Fulvia said goodbye to her husband for the last time as he sailed off to Sicily as Caesar's choice to replace Cato as governor there. This was an important appointment: possession of the island was critical for controlling movement between the eastern and western Mediterranean, and Sicily provided much of the grain consumed at Rome and elsewhere in Italy.

Curio's service, however, was cut short. In the early summer, he was sent to deal with forces loyal to Pompey in North Africa. He led a fleet and two legions across the Mediterranean from Sicily to Utica, where he engaged the Pompeian commander, Attius Varus, and his powerful ally, King Juba of Numidia. Curio enjoyed some initial successes, but ultimately his rashness and overconfidence led him into an ambush, where he was surrounded by Juba's cavalry, considered by the Romans to be

---

38. Cicero's anxieties are revealed in letters to Atticus (*Att.* 7.10–14 = *SBA* 133–8) and Terentia and Tullia themselves (*Fam.* 14.18 and 14 = *SBF* 144–5). See also Treggiari 2007: 100–17.

the best in the world. Curio died fighting. One source reports that his severed head was delivered to Juba.[39]

Antonius

The final showdown of the civil war happened later that summer, when Caesar definitively defeated the bulk of the republican forces in a battle near the city of Pharsalus in northern Greece. Pompey fled, seeking refuge with Ptolemy XIII, the child-king of Egypt, whose father had been Pompey's longtime ally. The young Ptolemy and his advisors quickly grasped that Caesar's goodwill was more valuable than honoring the previous king's allegiances, so he decapitated Pompey as soon as the general landed on Egyptian soil.[40]

Caesar's fight with Pompey was over, but the republican cause was not dead. The war would continue for much of the next four years in the east, in North Africa, and in Spain. Caesar spent so much time stamping out the remnants of republican resistance that, between his victory in 49 and his death in 44, the dictator (for that is what he now was) was rarely in Rome. His first return to Rome after Pharsalus was delayed for two years, first by a lengthy dalliance with Cleopatra in Egypt. He helped her defeat Ptolemy XIII, her younger brother and former husband (following Egyptian tradition), and then took up with her himself. Their affair resulted in a son named Caesarion. Eventually, however, duty called, and Caesar departed for a lightning-quick march northward to the kingdom of Pontus, on the south shore of the Black Sea, where in a mere five days he defeated King Pharnaces, who had taken advantage of the Romans' civil war to expand his own territory. Caesar's victory was so swift that he immortalized it with his most famous quip, "I came, I saw, I conquered" (*veni, vidi, vici*). Then word reached Caesar that Antonius, who had been with Caesar at Pharsalus but who had been sent back to Italy after Pompey's death, had completely lost control of the situation there: there were riots and revolt, legions mutinied, and the whole peninsula was in financial crisis. It was, at long last, time to go home and right the ship of state.

---

39. App., *B Civ.* 2.44–5. This detail is not included in Caesar's account of the battle (*B Civ.* 2.42) or in Cass. Dio's (41.42).
40. Plut., *Vit. Pomp.* 77.1–88.6.

FIGURE 3.1. Bust of Antonius, Museo Arqueológico Nacional, Madrid.
Source: agefotostock / Alamy Stock Photo.

Administration was clearly not Antonius's strong suit: he had built his reputation on the battlefield. Fulvia's third husband was daring, courageous, and famously handsome (Figure 3.1, a bust of Antonius dated to his lifetime), with an appearance that some said proved his family's claim that they were descended from Hercules himself. Born in 83 BCE,[41] he was the scion of two of Rome's most prominent aristocratic clans—his grandfather brought the Antonian family to real prominence in 102 BCE with a swift and successful assignment against the pirates that prowled the Mediterranean (Figure 3.2, the *gens Antonia*). He followed that up

---

41. Plutarch is unsure whether the year of Antonius's birth is either 86 or 83, but the latter fits somewhat better with his political career (Plut., *Ant.* 86.8 with Pelling 1988, *ad loc.*). After his death, Antonius was subject to *damnatio memoriae*, an officially sanctioned destruction or removal of all memorials of him, and his birthday was declared to be ill-omened (Cass. Dio, 51.19.3). On Antonius's birthday, p. 110. See Rüpke 2011, 151–2 and Lange 2009, 136–40.

with a consulship three years later. The next generation was less respectable. Antonius's uncle, Gaius, was expelled from the Senate in 70 BCE for reprehensible treatment of Rome's allies in Greece, refusal to recognize the judgment in a court case that had gone against him, and excessive debt.[42] This same man recovered from this temporary setback, eventually holding the consulship alongside Cicero, who offered him the rich province of Macedonia in exchange for his compliance in the suppression of Catiline's conspiracy. Gaius Antonius went on to prove that he had not learned much from his earlier troubles: he was later convicted of extortion for his exploitation of the province. Antonius's father held a command against the pirates two decades after his own father's successful campaign, but his results were considerably less stellar. At least he had married well: Antonius's mother was a Julia, a distant cousin of Caesar and a woman renowned for her outstanding valor.[43]

Antonius had early on shown ambition and promise. At the ripe old age of twenty-five, he was offered a civilian post on the staff of the new Roman governor of Syria. Plutarch says that Antonius refused the invitation until he was offered the position of cavalry prefect.[44] He quickly proved himself able and audacious in combat. His next post was with Caesar in Gaul, where he remained for several years, returning to Rome in 53 to seek his first elected office.

Antonius, also from an early age, had earned himself a reputation for fast living, like his friend, Curio: too much wine, too many lovers, and not enough cash to cover his lavish lifestyle. He maintained a scandalous, long-term relationship with Fadia, the daughter of a wealthy former slave and the mother of some of Antonius's children.[45] No matter how wealthy her father was, however, in the opinion of Rome's elite, Fadia's riches were insufficient to compensate for the stain of her social status.

Other notorious affairs followed. Antonius took up with Cytheris, an actress who had been a slave. Her former owner, P. Volumnius Eutrapelus, was a man of equestrian rank, wickedly witty,[46] wealthy, and well-respected enough to associate with Rome's political elite. Cicero

---

42. Asc. 84C.
43. Plut., *Ant.* 1–2.
44. Plut., *Ant.* 3.1.
45. Cic., *Phil.* 2.3 and 13.23 with *Att.* 16.11.1 = *SBA* 420.1.
46. Cic. *Fam.* 7.32 = SB 113.

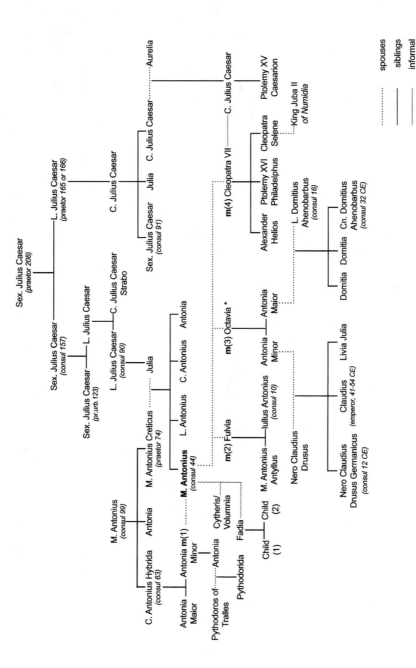

* reference Fulvia's family tree

FIGURE 3.2. The *gens Antonia* (J. Jeffs).

and Atticus were his close friends, as was Caesar. After Caesar's assassination, Eutrapelus transferred his loyalty to Antonius, with whom he went on to serve as *praefectus fabrum,* a senior aide-de-camp.[47]

Eutrapelus passed his beautiful slave around to his powerful friends. Cytheris's sexual entanglements will have helped ensure Eutrapelus's access to the highest echelons of Roman society. He gave her a name to reflect her physical charms: the name "Cytheris" alludes to the Greek goddess Aphrodite who was thought to have arisen from the sea near the island of Cythera. Once Cytheris gained her freedom, her official name became Volumnia, the feminine form of Eutrapelus's clan name. Her former slave-name became her cognomen (nickname).

After obtaining her freedom, Volumnia seems to have used Cytheris as her stage name. She made her living as a *mima*,[48] an actress who performed in mimes. These were not the silent performances we call by that name today, but rather were a ribald type of theatrical entertainment that combined singing, dancing, and acting. Despite the enormous popularity of their performances among the people of Rome, including the upper classes, mime actors, as was the case for most types of public entertainers, were viewed by freeborn Romans, especially aristocrats, with a certain amount of distaste. Mime actresses—indeed, actresses of any type—were often slaves, and almost by definition they were thought to be loose women: they performed without a mask and were scantily clad. No proper lady would ever, under any circumstances, risk her reputation by associating with such people, let alone perform in a mime. This is, of course, why Cicero, in two different courtroom attacks on Fulvia's former sister-in-law, Clodia, insinuates that she, too, worked in the theater.[49]

Volumnia is also identified by our sources as a courtesan,[50] and she was tied romantically not just to Antonius (we can date their relationship to the late 50s and early 40s, ending only with his marriage to Fulvia),[51] but also Brutus, the future assassin of Caesar, and the poet Gallus, whom she is said to have thrown over for Antonius and who dedicated four books of love poetry to her, calling her by the cryptonym Lycoris. To be desirable to such men, Volumnia must have been refined,

---

47. Cic., *Phil.* 13.3. Nep., *Att.* 9.4, 10.2, and 12.4.
48. [Aur. Vict.] *De vir. ill.* 82.2.
49. *Sest.* 116 and *Cael.* 64 with Skinner 2011: 96–120.
50. Serv., ad *Ecl.* 10.1.
51. Cic., *Att.* 10.10.5 and 10.16.5 = *SBA* 201.5 and 208.5.

talented, and clever, as well as physically attractive. Cicero found her presence at a dinner party at Eutrapelus's home—and the fact that she reclined on a dining couch with her patron rather than sitting upright as proper women should do—scandalous and a little intimidating. He wrote to his friend, Papirius, that Papirius should not be shocked that he had attended such an event. He had not known Cytheris (he calls her by her old slave name as an insult) was going to be there, and besides, he was not really interested in that sort of thing.[52]

Volumnia's relationships with the members of Rome's elite may well have begun while she was still a slave, perhaps performing for them as a child at dinner parties: tombstones from the Roman world make it clear that many actresses began their careers early in life. At that time, Eutrapelus may have also indulged his friends' desires to sample her considerable charms. Even after she was no longer his slave, Volumnia was required to fulfill her continuing obligation to her former owner by obliging his companions.[53]

Whether one addressed her as Volumnia or Cytheris could imply respect or disdain. Cicero accused Antonius of humiliating local dignitaries when she accompanied him on business throughout Italy by demanding that they address her as Volumnia.[54] Cicero himself usually calls her Cytheris, as he did in his letter to Papirius. The exception is a reference in a letter to his wife, Terentia,[55] where he refers to her as Volumnia, partly because he is addressing Terentia, a matron of impeccable propriety, and partly because he and Terentia were at the moment dependent on Volumnia's goodwill. This was in early January of 47. The civil war between Caesar and Pompey was over, but Caesar had still not permitted Cicero to return to Rome. Terentia had apparently asked Volumnia to intercede with Antonius on Cicero's behalf. Terentia's letter about their meeting is lost, but we can reconstruct from Cicero's response that Volumnia had behaved presumptuously, although ultimately she seems to have been receptive to Terentia's plea. Cicero complains, however, that Volumnia performed her mission with insufficient caution and care.

Antonius's relationships with Fadia and Volumnia were a political liability; in an effort to scandalize other senators, Cicero claimed

---

52. Cic., *Fam.* 9.26 = SB *Fam.* 197.
53. Traina 2001, 88–91; Keith 2011: 38–40.
54. Cic., *Phil.* 2.58.
55. Cic., *Fam.* 14.16 = *SBF* 163.

they were legal marriages.[56] Yet, lower-status lovers aside, Antonius ran with the fashionable crowd of the day: Curio, Caelius, Gaius Cornelius Dolabella (who was briefly married to Tullia, Cicero's daughter), and his own younger brothers, Gaius and Lucius. Clodius was part of this circle, too, even though he was about a decade older than the rest. We know that his association with Antonius ended dramatically when, in 53 in the midst of Clodius's escalating conflict with Milo, Clodius was physically attacked by Antonius in the Forum. It is not clear what the fight was about, but some have alleged that, already at that early date, Antonius had a liaison with Fulvia. That is unlikely, however, since Cicero implies, in his defense speech on behalf of Milo delivered the next year, that there had been a political break between the men.[57]

A Third Marriage

Whether or not they had a dalliance some years before, Antonius and Fulvia married in 47, a few months after she emerged from mourning for Curio and after Antonius divorced his wife (and first cousin), Antonia, with whom he had a daughter, also named Antonia.[58] There were rumors that Antonius suspected Antonia of an affair with Dolabella, who was at that time still married (albeit unhappily) to Cicero's daughter, Tullia. The new match with Fulvia seems to have been a good one that helped Antonius refrain from some of his more reprehensible behavior. Some have thought that Caesar himself may have arranged the match.[59] Political considerations were surely factored in: Fulvia remained the most visible reminder of the late Clodius. Her new husband could, as Curio had before him, lay claim to the support of the urban plebs.[60]

---

56. *Phil.* 2.3 and 20. Some scholars accept the historicity of the marriage to Fadia (e.g., Harders 2019, 121; Rizzelli 2006; Kleiner 1992, 358; Huzar 1985, 97–8; Johnson 1972–1973, 21).

57. Cic., *Mil.* 40. Babcock (1965, 12 and 16–17) accepts as fact an affair between Antonius and Fulvia while she was still married to Clodius, but most scholars dismiss Cicero's later insinuation (*Phil.* 2.21 combined with 48–9) as slander devised to serve his rhetorical purpose.

58. The date of Antonia's divorce is assured by *Phil.* 2.99. Marriages between close cousins were not common in Rome, but neither were they stigmatized among aristocratic families in the Late Republic. Other examples are not far to seek: we can point to the marriage of Clodia to her first cousin, Q. Caecilius Metellus. Babcock's notion that Fulvia pressured Antonius into divorcing Antonia is only speculation (1965, 13)

59. Dolabella's alleged affair with Antonia: Cic., *Phil.* 2.99 and Plut., *Vit. Ant.* 9.1–2. Fulvia as positive influence: Plut., *Vit. Ant.* 10.2–3.

60. Welch 1995, 192.

Fulvia was a stabilizing influence, and she seems to have inspired Antonius to strive for respectability. Cicero tells a story (perhaps of his own manufacture) of how Antonius revealed to Fulvia that he was ending his affair with Volumnia. When returning to Rome in either December of 47 or January of 46, Antonius disguised his appearance and pretended to be a messenger carrying a love letter to Fulvia, who was waiting for Antonius at home. As she read the letter, she wept with joy when he swore off any future assignations with his longtime lover. Able to bear his secret no longer, Antonius revealed himself and was met with a passionate embrace. Cicero tells the tale to paint Antonius as weak, effeminate, and unduly beholden to a woman, but the story (if it is true) reveals a playful side to Antonius's personality and shows real tenderness between him and Fulvia.[61]

Antonius, Fulvia, and their growing brood set up house. Since children of divorced Roman parents generally resided with their father, Antonia likely joined her half- and step- siblings in their new home. In addition to Claudius, Claudia, and the young Curio, there were soon two new brothers. The older boy, as was standard practice at Rome at the time, as Antonius's first-born legitimate son, was named Marcus Antonius. The child was given the nickname Antyllus, in honor of Anto, the mythical son of Hercules who was supposedly the founder of the Antonian clan.[62] His younger brother, born sometime shortly after Caesar's assassination, bore the highly unusual first name of Iullus, unprecedented in both Fulvia's and Antonius's families. It was a strategic choice, intended to shore up Antonius's claim to being Julius Caesar's political (if not legal) heir in the aftermath of his death.

The house where the new family settled was a real conversation piece for its appearance, location, and the scandalous circumstances through which Antonius came to own it. In the aftermath of Caesar's victory at Pharsalus, many of his friends back in Rome had scooped up, at rock bottom prices, property that had belonged to Pompey's supporters. Antonius had been the only bidder at the auction of Pompey's estate, and he paid a mere fraction of what the late general's houses and gardens were worth. The centerpiece of it all was a house in the Campus Martius, a low-lying area along the Tiber River, just west of the Palatine and Capitoline Hills. The house was stately and tastefully appointed,

---

61. Ending relationship with Cytheris: Cic., *Phil.* 2.69 and 77. Cf. Plut., *Vit. Ant.* 10.4.
62. Plut., *Vit. Ant.* 4.1.

luxurious but not overly so. It was part of the complex that included Rome's first permanent stone theater and a portico large enough to house a meeting of the full senate. It was Pompey's great gift to the people of Rome. The house was so distinctive that ancient writers continued to describe it for us, and for centuries it would convey the power and dominance of its owners.[63] When Antonius acquired the house, Caesar was the only Roman more powerful than he.

Along with the house came Pompey's wine collection, his elegant silver dining service, couches, and tapestries. Antonius, a man famous for his extravagant tastes, is said to have wondered how Pompey could have dined in so modest a home. The most impressive element of the house greeted visitors as soon as they entered the front vestibule: mounted on the walls were the beaks of pirate ships that Pompey had captured in his wildly successful campaign against the pirates in 67 BCE. Cicero later accused Antonius of pretending that the ships' beaks were a memorial of his grandfather's and father's service to Rome.

Everything Changes in a Moment

Antonius's position in Roman society had, for the last few years, depended on the favor shown to him by Caesar. Falling out of favor, as happened when Antonius failed to control Italy and Rome while Caesar was in the east, had severe consequences, including the loss of his position as Caesar's master of horse, the title given to a dictator's second-in-command.[64] At that point, in 46, Antonius and Fulvia disappear from the historical record until October 45, when Caesar returned to Rome again after defeating republican forces in Spain. All the leading men of Rome headed north to escort the dictator back to Rome, but Antonius was singled out for the special honor of riding back to the city in Caesar's carriage. After arriving home, Caesar was appointed consul for 44 (genuine elections were no longer held). He chose Antonius as his colleague. The fates of the two men were from that point on inextricably intertwined, but not in the way it must have seemed at the time.

---

63. Plut., *Vit. Pomp.* 40.5 with Cic., *Phil.* 2.64–9. Russell 2016: 156–62.

64. An alternate interpretation of Antonius's relationship to Caesar in 46–45, wherein Antonius was not estranged from Caesar but merely reassigned to deal with pressing financial matters, is offered in Ramsey 2004.

Caesar's return to Rome in 45 was to be his last. While in the city, he focused his energies on stabilizing the empire through extensive administrative reforms, including replenishing and expanding the membership of the senate, whose ranks had been decimated by the civil war. This move not only restored the senate to full working capacity, but also populated it with people who owed their advancement to Caesar. His ambitious building programs beautified the city and provided employment for many of Rome's poor, a necessary step since he also cut in half the number of city residents who qualified for free grain distributions. Other poor citizens and many of Caesar's veterans found employment in the twenty colonies he established throughout the empire.

The value of Caesar's efforts to set Rome on a firm foundation were, in the eyes of many, overshadowed by his increasingly authoritarian behavior, particularly toward members of the senate. The Romans had long prided themselves on expelling the kings that tradition said had ruled the city for its first two and a half centuries. They had, for hundreds of years, carefully avoided the consolidation of too much power in the hands of a single individual, a value most clearly visible in the Roman insistence that every magistrate, especially those with military power, have a colleague and be responsible to the senate. But now Caesar acted as though he was not subject to the senate's authority. If the senators wanted to work with him, fine. If not, he would proceed on his own. Caesar began to do things like issue "decrees of the senate" on his own initiative. Cicero reported that his name had shown up as a signatory on some decrees that, so far as he knew, had not even been debated in the senate. Caesar seemed to revel in most of the kingly honors heaped upon him: a golden chair to use in senate meetings, the right to wear a purple toga any time he wished, the insertion of his name among the gods listed in public prayers—just to name a few.[65]

Everyone knew that discontent was growing, even Caesar. Cicero once called on Caesar at his home and, despite being a former consul and Caesar's elder, Cicero was made to sit in the atrium of the house and wait for an audience, just like everyone else. It was reported to Cicero that Caesar had said, "I have no doubt that I am a most hated man, since Marcus Cicero sits waiting and cannot see me at his own convenience. I mean, if anyone is easygoing, he is. Even so, I do not doubt that he

---

65. Honors for Caesar: Cass. Dio 44.4.1–8.4; App., *B Civ.* 2.106–7. False decrees of the senate: Cic., *Fam.* 9.15.4–5 = *SBF* 196.4–5.

loathes me." Caesar let it be known that he knew his life was in danger. Cicero, who had returned from the Civil War only because of Caesar's mercy toward his former opponents, openly addressed the issue in a fawning speech delivered in a senate meeting, reassuring Caesar that no one was so brazen and deranged as to threaten his life, on which all of Rome depended.[66] Caesar seems to have thought that the hostility from the city's elite was personal. He did not understand that, for many, it stemmed from anger over the deterioration of Rome's republican form of government. The final straw seems to have been his taking up the title of dictator-for-life in early winter of 44.[67] Rome had its first king in almost 500 years.

Caesar's Assassination

In addition to all the other tasks before him in the winter of 45–44, Caesar was preparing for a major military expedition against the Parthian Empire, which sat at Rome's eastern border, beyond the province of Syria. The Parthians, who controlled the territory between the Euphrates and Indus rivers, had clashed with Rome before, most recently in 53 BCE, when Caesar's former ally, Crassus, had been utterly defeated at the battle of Carrhae.

On the morning of March 15, 44 BCE, three days before his planned departure, Caesar headed to a meeting of the senate. He arrived late: he had not been feeling well and had thought simply to skip the meeting, but he was persuaded to go by someone who knew what awaited him in the colonnade of Pompey's theater, where the senate was meeting that day. Upon his arrival, Caesar was met by a crowd of friends and supporters, including Antonius. Someone, a Greek named Artemidorus, tried to pass Caesar a note, warning him of what was about to happen, but the crowd pressed Caesar forward, toward the theater, before he could read what had been handed to him. He paused, however, for a moment when he caught sight of a seer named Spurinna, who had earlier warned him to beware the Ides of March, as the day was called. Caesar chided the man that the Ides had come and that he was still in fine health. Spurinna

---

66. Cic., *Att.* 14.1.2 = *SBA* 355.2; *Marcell.* 21–26.
67. Certainly by the festival of the Lupercalia on February 15: Cic., *Phil.* 2.87 and Joseph., *AJ* 14.211–12.

conceded the point—the Ides had indeed come—but, he noted, they had not yet gone.

Caesar was then swept into the theater by the crowd. Someone of the conspirators approached Antonius and asked to have a word with him, detaching him from Caesar's entourage. Caesar entered the theater on his own. Soon shouts rang out, and senators stampeded out of the meeting. Caesar lay on the floor of the colonnade, at the very foot of Pompey's statue. Bleeding from twenty-three stab wounds, Caesar gasped his last.[68]

The conspiracy to assassinate Caesar had as many as sixty members. Some, like the group's leaders, Marcus Junius Brutus and Gaius Cassius Longinus, were former enemies whom Caesar had pardoned. Others had long been loyal supporters who could no longer bear Caesar's increasingly kingly behavior. The majority of the group had wanted to assassinate Antonius, too, as the obvious heir to Caesar's power, but Brutus had forbidden it. Brutus's decision had unforeseen consequences for everyone, not the least of whom were Fulvia and her children.

---

68. The tale is told with great drama by Plut., *Vit. Caes.* 61.1–66.14.

4

Fulvia's Final Act

The attack on Caesar in the senate meeting on the Ides of March, 44 BCE, was an event of seismic proportions: it set in motion a series of events, many epic in their own right, that would turn Rome from a republic into an empire over the course of thirteen years. The period between the dictator's murder and the moment when only one of the generals who fought to succeed him was left standing in 31 BCE is commonly called the triumviral period, after the group of three men (triumvirs) who dominated politics: Octavian, Lepidus, and Antonius.

The consequences of Caesar's death for Fulvia were dramatic and instantaneous. Although she had spent her entire life as a member of Rome's elite, Fulvia had never been in the glare of the political spotlight in quite the same way as she would within a few hours after Caesar's death, when Antonius stepped forward to fill the power vacuum in the city. The glare followed her until her own demise a few years later. She is more visible in the ancient accounts of the late 40s BCE than she is for any other period of her life, and we know more about her activities in 44–40 than we do of any other woman at Rome in those years.

Unfortunately, the basic facts lie underneath a thick layer of hostile interpretation and embellishment. It is a truism that history is written by the victors; there is no denying that Fulvia was on the losing side. All the sources are hostile to her. The worst portrays her as a caricature of a woman overstepping the bounds of proper matronal behavior, describing her as having nothing feminine about her except her physical form (*nihil muliebre praeter corpus gerens*).[1] Another claims that

---

1. Vell. Pat. 2.74.2–3; but compare Orosius, who says that she exercised her dominance "like a woman" (*ut mulier*), 6.18.17.

Fulvia. Celia E. Schultz, Oxford University Press. © Oxford University Press 2021.
DOI: 10.1093/oso/9780190697136.003.0004

Cleopatra, Antonius's last and most infamous romantic partner, owed Fulvia a debt of gratitude because Fulvia had trained him to be subservient to women.[2]

By now, there should be no doubt that Fulvia was a strong woman, capable of independent and politically savvy action. She had demonstrated as much almost a decade before, in the aftermath of Clodius's murder. But the twisted version of her preserved by the sources was created by Cicero and by supporters of Octavian, Caesar's great-nephew who defeated Antonius in the final round of the Republic's civil wars—and by Antonius and Octavian themselves. Our sources emphasize that both men had much to gain by pinning responsibility for the bloodiest and most embarrassing episodes of this period on her.[3] Their reconciliation, after her death in 40 BCE, would look more genuine if Fulvia were responsible for the armed conflict that arose between Octavian and Antonius's supporters the year before. The accounts we have are dependent on a variety of earlier sources that are no longer extant, the most influential of which was the autobiography of Octavian, written later in his life, after he had become Augustus, Rome's first emperor. It is clear from what little of the work survives that Augustus recounted his rise to power in a way that made himself seem destined to rule, the perfect embodiment of *pietas* (a particularly Roman form of dutifulness) toward Julius Caesar and the Roman people, a relentless avenger of Caesar's murder, and a man blameless for the ugliness of the triumviral period. As we might expect, Fulvia and Antonius come across as villains in most of the ancient sources.[4] These biases have to be identified carefully and disengaged whenever possible.

Shifting Alliances and Stabilizing the City

As Caesar gasped his last on the floor of the meeting hall in Pompey's theater complex, the senators scattered as quickly as they could. The conspirators had completely misjudged how their colleagues would

---

2. Plut., *Vit. Ant.* 10.3.
3. Both Octavian and Antonius will have had incentive to inflate her role in the Perusine War: App., *B Civ.* 5.59; Plut., *Vit. Ant.* 30.2–3; Cass. Dio 48.28.3; Roddaz 1988, 318; Delia 1991, 204.
4. The main sources for the triumviral period are Cass. Dio, Books 44–50 and App., *B Civ.* 3–5. supplemented by several of Plutarch's *Lives*. Cicero's letters cease in June of 43; he was dead by late autumn of that same year.

react: they seem to have expected that others would see the assault on the dictator as an act to free the Republic from a tyrant and then rush to their aid. Instead, there was a stampede out of the building, followed by panic and looting in the streets as senators ran home for protection. The presence of armed gladiators in the theater that day added to the chaos, although it is not clear if they had been brought in by the conspirators as extra muscle or if they were there to practice for a performance. Antonius, who had been waylaid by one of the conspirators before the attack on Caesar, assumed that he was intended as their next victim. He raced home to Fulvia and the children, stripping off his consul's toga as he went in order to escape notice. One source says he put on a slave's clothing and hid for a time.[5] Once safe at home, he ordered the household staff to prepare for an attack.

The attack never came. The conspirators and some of the gladiators withdrew from the low-lying area of the theater to the summit of the nearby Capitoline Hill, the site of many sacred temples, and stayed there. The choice was strategic: the hill sits between the Campus Martius, where Pompey's theater lay, and the Forum, the political heart of the city. Because it is protected on three sides by sheer cliffs, access to the fortified citadel at the top was restricted. By the next day,[6] the Forum was filled with soldiers, brought in from just outside the city where they had gathered for Caesar to lead them against the Parthians three days after the Ides. They were commanded by Lepidus, Caesar's master of horse, who had dined with him just the night before his death. For the moment, a tense calm held the city.

A group of Caesar's former soldiers and close associates gathered in the Forum. Lepidus advocated for punishing the assassins, but Antonius disagreed. As people came to realize that the conspirators were not intent on widespread murder and mayhem, public sentiment toward them warmed. Moving against Brutus and Cassius could cause a public backlash. On the second morning after the assassination, in his capacity as consul, Antonius summoned the senate to the temple of Tellus (the Earth) near one of his homes in the Carinae neighborhood of the Esquiline Hill. Cicero, speaking for the many senators who had been dismayed by Caesar's increasingly autocratic behavior, delivered an impassioned speech in favor of amnesty for the assassins, and it was

---

5. Plut., *Vit. Ant.* 14.1. Cf. App., *B Civ.* 2.118 and Cass. Dio 44.22.2.
6. The exact sequence of events is not entirely clear. I follow the reconstruction laid out in Pelling 1988, 150–1.

agreed that they should be invited to parley. The message was relayed, and Cassius agreed to meet on the condition that Antonius and Lepidus send hostages. Lepidus sent his young son.[7] The boy was the nephew of the two men who led the conspiracy. His mother, Junia, was the sister of Brutus; Junia's sister was married to Cassius. Antonius sent his son, Antyllus, who cannot have been more than three years old. That night, a little more than forty-eight hours after Caesar's death, Brutus dined at the house of Lepidus, his brother-in-law, while Cassius was Antonius's guest. As the lady of the house, Fulvia would have taken on the arrangements for dinner with the man who determined whether her child would safely return to her.

In the following weeks, the city experienced a precarious peace. At the meeting at the Temple of Tellus, the first order of business was to stabilize the situation. The senate had settled on a compromise: Caesar would not be declared a tyrant, and no steps would be taken to prosecute those who had killed him. The further decision that his decrees and laws would remain in place meant that the return to traditional institutions was delayed: Caesar had appointed magistrates for the next three years, so there would be no elections for at least that long. It also meant that both the leading Caesarians and the leading conspirators all maintained the powerful positions the dictator had given them. Antonius and his colleague Dolabella were confirmed in their consulships for 44 and Decimus Brutus, one of the conspirators, would be consul in 42. Brutus, Cassius, and Antonius's younger brother, Gaius, were to continue serving as praetors for 44. The youngest Antonius brother, Lucius, was a tribune of the plebs. For the time being, they all had to work alongside one another. At the end of their current terms, however, all of these men except Lucius would take up the powerful provinces they had earlier been assigned. This meant that in the year 43, each of them would have an army.

Now the leading man in Rome, Antonius was in a difficult position. The assassins had significant support in the senate, and few could countenance more violence. Peace had to be maintained. Yet Antonius's personal opinion seems to have aligned more closely with Caesar's veterans, whose anger was directed at Brutus, Cassius, and their followers. At Caesar's funeral, Antonius swayed the people of the city, whose reaction

---

7. Lepidus's son may have been a teenager, but it is more likely that he was younger, perhaps only ten or eleven. Treggiari (2019, 135) puts his parents' marriage in the very late 60s or early 50s; Münzer (1999, 272) proposes a birth date in 55 BCE.

to the murder had been somewhat muted thus far (if not actually favorable toward the assassins), to anger and grief over Caesar's death. Their upset turned to rage when it was revealed that, in his will, Caesar had left his gardens for their benefit and that he had set aside funds to be distributed among them. Brutus, Cassius, and their allies understood Antonius's actions, which shored up his own position and protected Caesar's memory, as hostile to themselves. They were not wrong: within a few weeks of the assassination, Brutus and Cassius had been stripped of the provinces allotted to them for the following year.

The Heir Arrives

The situation became even more complicated for everyone, but especially for Antonius, less than a month after Caesar's death. Eighteen-year-old Gaius Octavius arrived in Italy from Greece, where he had been studying. He was the dead man's great-nephew and the heir to the bulk of Caesar's estate. Not the least of the benefits this bestowed upon the young man was a powerful new name. Following Roman custom, he took on the name of his benefactor and added his original clan name as an adjective at the end. Thus Gaius Octavius became Gaius Julius Caesar Octavianus, known in history books today as Octavian—at least until he became the Emperor Augustus. Cicero, writing to his friend Atticus on April 11 of that year, gleefully imagined the meeting between Octavian and Antonius, who had been charged with executing Caesar's will: Would people rally around the young man? Would Antonius accuse him of whipping up the opposition? Probably not, Cicero decided. He thought it would amount to nothing.[8] That would prove to be one of the most stunning miscalculations of Cicero's political career.

Octavian arrived in Italy with remarkable speed after receiving word of Caesar's death, probably helped along by his great-uncle's powerful allies, who seized upon him as a possible counterweight to Antonius. Antonius had long been a controversial figure, and his track record as a magistrate was not good. In addition, many in Rome accused him of manufacturing decrees supposedly issued by Caesar: in the immediate aftermath of the assassination, Caesar's widow, Calpurnia, had turned over to Antonius the dictator's papers and seal. A suspicious number

---

8. Cic., *Att.* 14.5.3 = SBA 359.3.

of previously unissued decrees were "discovered" in the days and weeks after the Ides of March. Some months later, in a series of scathing speeches, Cicero repeatedly insinuated that Fulvia was involved in Antonius's backroom dealings and pay-to-play method of running the state.[9]

As soon as he heard the news of Caesar's death, Octavian departed Greece, where he had been waiting for his great-uncle to collect him on his way east for the Parthian campaign. The young man reached Rome in the second week of April.[10] One suspects this caught Antonius off guard. He appears to have already bruited it about that the heir had declined his inheritance, which, if true, would have meant that Antonius and the conspirator Decimus would share the estate between them as heirs in the second degree. But Octavian, bolstered by the enthusiastic reception he received from Caesar's soldiers and from the people in general as he made his way to Rome, made his claim upon the estate in front of Gaius Antonius, who had replaced Brutus as urban praetor. More threatening to Antonius were the moves Octavian took to have himself legally recognized as Caesar's adopted son, which required passage of a special law. Antonius had worked to present himself as heir to Caesar's power, and Octavian was clearly positioning himself to do the same. Antonius thwarted Octavian's efforts—but only for a time.

Antonius Becomes the Target

It was clear to everyone that the situation was untenable and that war would come again. In a letter from November of 44, Cicero confided to his friend, Atticus, "Octavian expects that there will be war against Antonius, with himself in command. So I expect that in a few days we will be in arms."[11] Cicero was right on this point. Popular anger against the conspirators and dissatisfaction with Antonius for not punishing them—and for his increasingly autocratic behavior—had been growing for months. Soon after the assassination, Brutus and Cassius withdrew from Rome but stayed relatively close by. Later in the summer, they issued an edict declaring that, because they had been prevented from

---

9. Caesar's papers: Plut., *Vit. Ant.* 15.1–3. Insinuations about Fulvia: Cic., *Phil.* 2.95, 3.10, and 5.11.
10. For a detailed reconstruction of Octavian's itinerary during his first weeks in Italy, see Toher 2004.
11. Cic., *Att.* 16.8.1 = *SBA* 418.1.

performing the duties of their public offices, they were laying down those offices and entering self-imposed exile in order to keep the peace. They headed to the provinces that Caesar had originally assigned to them, but which had been taken away by Antonius.

By August, Brutus was in Athens, ostensibly to study philosophy but in reality to gather forces and to build a war chest to enable him to take his original province, Macedonia, from its new governor for 43, Gaius Antonius. Cassius headed first to Asia and by the beginning of 43, he arrived in Syria, where the current governor and the governor of neighboring Bithynia turned their provinces over to him. Decimus Brutus, another leading conspirator, had already taken up his appointed province of Cisalpine Gaul, even though the senate had removed it from his control on June 1 and had handed it over—at least on paper—to Antonius himself.

Meanwhile, the relationship between Antonius and Octavian continued to deteriorate, despite efforts to maintain the appearance of civility between them. Antonius, as the senior statesman, sitting consul, and military hero, would seem to have had the upper hand, but Octavian's popularity was growing. He had also found eager allies among those in the senate, led by Cicero, who intended to play him against Antonius. The end to any pretense of reconciliation between the great orator, whose sympathies lay with the conspirators, and Antonius came in September, when Cicero delivered the first in a series of blistering speeches against Antonius, called the Philippics, after an earlier series of hostile speeches by the Greek orator Demosthenes against King Philip II of Macedonia. At issue in the first speech was Antonius's public complaint that Cicero had shirked his duties by not appearing at a meeting of the senate at which further honors for the deceased Caesar were to be debated. Cicero responded by urging Antonius and his consular colleague, Dolabella (Cicero's former son-in-law), to return their focus to the welfare of the Roman people.

Cicero maintained favorable relations with Octavian through the autumn of that year, although it is clear from his letters to Atticus that as 44 BCE drew to a close, he had come to see "the boy," as he disparagingly refers to him, as a threat almost equal to that posed by Antonius.[12] The only one removed from the frequent repositioning and realignment of loyalties was Lepidus, whose troops had helped Antonius bring calm

---

12. See esp. *Att.* 16.9, 11, 14, 15 = *SBA* 419, 420, 425, 426.

to the city in the immediate aftermath of Caesar's assassination. He had been out of Rome for some months, overseeing his provinces of Gaul and Spain, where he had been working, at Antonius's urging, to reconcile Sextus Pompey, the son of Pompey the Great and leader of a remnant of the republican forces, to Antonius and himself.[13] They were eager to ensure that Sextus and his forces did not take up the cause of the senate in the coming conflict.

The hostility that had been simmering in Rome just below the surface boiled over in October of 44, and Fulvia witnessed the event. Although it was a long-established republican tradition that Roman matrons did not accompany their husbands on military business, in the late Republic this began to change. For example, we know that Antonius himself had been accompanied at least once before on official business by his mother and his mistress.[14] Increasingly, in times of civil strife, women traveled along with their husbands rather than stay at home, alone and vulnerable to their political enemies.[15] So it was that Fulvia sought to escape the increasing tension and instability in the city by accompanying Antonius to the port city of Brundisium in the southeast corner of the peninsula, where Antonius intended to take command of four legions that had just returned from Macedonia, where they had been waiting to embark with Caesar on the Parthian campaign. Their new mission was to dislodge Decimus, who had been left, unmolested, in control of Cisalpine Gaul even though that provinces was now technically Antonius's.

The trip to Brundisium did not go as planned. Upon his arrival, Antonius discovered that the soldiers, who had already been complaining about Antonius's failure to act against the conspirators, had been approached by Octavian's agents. The soldiers took Antonius's offer of a donative of 100 *denarii* as an insult: Octavian's men had offered five times as much money. In a rage, Antonius ordered some of the men cut down. In his version of the tale, Cicero emphasizes Antonius's unhinged anger and the gory details: Fulvia's face was splashed with blood, the dying men laying at her husband's feet.[16]

The initial blood-letting seemed to have cowed the legions. Antonius planned to march with them northward along the peninsula's east coast

---

13. On the activities of Pompey's son in this period, see Welch 2012, 121–62.
14. Cic., *Phil.* 2.57–58; cf. 2.61.
15. Sextus Pompey's sister abandoned Rome with her brother: Suet., *Tib.* 6.3.
16. Cic., *Phil.* 3.4. See also Cass. Dio, 45.12.1–13.5. App., *B Civ.* 3.40–3, does not mention Fulvia's presence.

to Ariminum, where he would launch a campaign against Decimus, but another problem demanded immediate attention. Octavian had been gathering a military force of his own from among Caesar's veterans and his own supporters, despite holding no official position within the government. In mid-November, Antonius marched on Rome, and the city braced for bloodshed. Instead, Antonius's more moderate plan—to have Octavian declared an enemy of the state—was preempted by news that two of the Macedonian legions had defected to Octavian. Antonius decided to cut his losses. On November 28, Antonius, desperate to shore up the wavering support of Lepidus, persuaded the senate to declare a thanksgiving celebration in Lepidus's honor for his successful negotiations to reconcile Sextus. Later that same night, Antonius and his remaining troops departed for Gaul to take on Decimus Brutus. Octavian was still recruiting in the regions north of Rome.

While Antonius besieged Decimus at the Gallic city of Mutina (modern Modena), Cicero continued to rail against Antonius in the senate at Rome well into the spring of 43 BCE. The speeches, Philippics 3-14, are masterpieces of political invective—witty, caustic, forceful, with enough scandalous accusations and half-truths to keep their audience enthralled. When reading these speeches, it is important to bear in mind that Cicero treats the facts selectively and twists them to his advantage. He is free to hurl unfounded accusations of reprehensible public and private behavior: there were no libel laws in republican Rome. Very little of what he claims—especially about the women in Antonius's life—should be taken at face value. Yet, even so, we cannot ignore the Philippics. They are valuable historical sources: they proved instrumental in Cicero's campaign to erode the support for Antonius in the senate, to persuade that body to stand behind Decimus as the legitimate governor of Cisalpine Gaul, and to confirm Brutus as governor of Macedonia, Illyricum, and Greece. They also illustrate how a Roman politician might be attacked. Across the speeches, Cicero hits at Antonius everywhere he is vulnerable: his disloyalty to his commander and patron, his imperious behavior, the dubious legality of his actions, his mishandling of finances and unscrupulous accumulation of funds, his unsavory personal reputation, excessive violence, and even his home life.

Cicero made much of Antonius's reputation as a man of great passions: food, wine, and sex. Although there was no expectation that a Roman man would remain loyal to his wife (indeed Fulvia, like many women of her social class, probably expected that her husband would have lovers), the flamboyance of Antonius's love affairs made them a real political liability. Cicero scandalized his audience by claiming that Antonius had given Fadia and Volumnia undue privileges. Sexual liaisons with women of low social status were perfectly acceptable among Rome's elite; treating them as social equals was absolutely not. As was pointed out in the previous chapter,[17] Cicero implies that Antonius had legally married these two women, one the daughter of a former slave and the other a former slave herself. Both claims are fabrications intended to provoke shock and outrage. The orator goes even further, asserting that Antonius recognized Fadia's children as his own.[18] Cicero also chastised Antonius for flaunting his long relationship with Volumnia. Not only did she accompany Antonius as he traveled through Italy on official business, but she did so in an open litter, where everyone could see her, and (even more astonishing!) she rode ahead of Antonius's mother, who was relegated to a less prestigious position behind her in the train.[19] Antonius's wife at the time, his cousin Antonia, was apparently left behind at home—Cicero makes no mention of her.

While Cicero was whipping up opposition to Antonius in Rome, Antonius himself pressed the siege of Mutina in the winter of 44–43. Those working to counter Cicero's rhetorical offensive in the senate were aided by Antonius's mother, Julia (the late dictator's cousin), and Fulvia. The women pursued his interests—not in public view in the Forum, but in the private homes of leading families, places they had visited socially in happier circumstances. This was not unusual: when a man was not in Rome to defend himself, he relied on his allies, including the adult women in his life, to do that for him. The best documented instance of this is Cicero's wife, Terentia, who spent much of 58–57 lobbying Pompey (indirectly, of course) for Cicero's recall from exile and working to protect the family's property from the predations of his enemies, most prominently, Clodius.[20]

The historian Appian writes that, after Cicero delivered his Third and Fourth Philippics, two speeches demanding that Decimus be recognized as the legitimate representative of Rome in Gaul and that Antonius be declared an enemy of the state, on December 20, 44, the

17. See pp. 66–67.
18. Phil. 3.17 with 2.3.
19. See note 12.
20. Terentia's vigorous defense of Cicero's interests is reconstructed by Treggiari 2007, 56–77.

family took action: "Antonius' mother, wife, and son (him still just a boy), and his other relatives and friends spent the whole night going around to the houses of powerful men and pleading with them. In the morning, they threw themselves at the feet of those going to the senate house, wailing and lamenting, wearing mourning clothes and shouting. Some of the senators were moved by the sound and the sight and by so sudden a reversal of fortune."[21]

Appian has here heightened the drama of the story by collapsing the timeline: Antonius's family and friends had two weeks, not twelve hours, to make their case before the next meeting of the senate on January 1, 43. Still, it must have been a hectic and exhausting fortnight: the stakes were extremely high. Julia's and Fulvia's dramatic efforts, combined with arguments on behalf of Antonius made by his supporters in the senate, were successful, at least for the time being: Antonius would not be declared an enemy of Rome until April—a declaration that put Fulvia and her children in serious peril, both physical and financial. Once that declaration was made, Fulvia was swiftly beset by numerous lawsuits. Fortunately for her, Cicero's friend Atticus, a wealthy equestrian with powerful political connections, stepped in as her protector, despite his allegiance to Cicero and to Brutus. Atticus also worked to protect Antonius's friend and Volumnia's patron, Eutrapelus. Atticus's generosity paid off later, when Eutrapelus and Fulvia stepped in to protect Atticus from Antonius.[22]

As we have already seen with Cicero's deployment of Fadia and Volumnia as weapons against Antonius, wives and lovers were acceptable targets for political invective. Fulvia was no exception. Despite being a proper matron of aristocratic lineage, Fulvia catches the brunt of Cicero's anger in the Second Philippic, which was never delivered as a speech but circulated as a lengthy pamphlet, and in the Third Phillipic, the first of those speeches delivered on December 20, 44, that sparked Fulvia's and Julia's lobbying efforts. The portrait the orator paints in these speeches, embellished by passing references in some of the other Philippics, has been the basis for the picture of Fulvia that has survived the ages.

Despite the enormous gulf in social status between Volumnia and Fulvia, Cicero is able to attack them on similar grounds of rank and

---

21. App., *B Civ.* 3.51.
22. Nepos, *Att.* 9.1–10.6.

sexuality. It is misleading to think of the Rome's aristocracy as a single class where all members ranked equally. In a society where holding political office was the *raison d'être* for the upper orders, a family like the Fulvian clan, which had not held the consulship for three generations (and for Fulvia's branch of the clan, perhaps even longer than that), was not on a par with those who had been in power more recently. Thus in the Third Philippic, Cicero is able to throw back at Antonius an attack Antonius had made on Octavian, who was at this point was still Cicero's ally: that the latter came from less exalted stock than the noble Antonian clan.[23] Octavian's mother (a relative of Caesar's!) may have come from the small town of Aricia, Cicero conceded, but her father reached the praetorship and her husband would have reached the consulship had he not died too young. Cicero went on to point out that Fulvia came from an equally small place—Tusculum—but her father was a man of paltry standing (*homo nullo numero*, "a man of no account") and her grandfather, though noble, was an eccentric who dressed up as an actor and scattered coins to the crowd. Fulvia's father was a genuine social liability: in the Second Philippic, Cicero snidely describes Fulvia's young son, sent to the conspirators as a hostage the night of the assassination, as "a noble child, the grandson of Marcus Bambalio."[24]

Cicero wields the status of Fulvia's family as a weapon to wound her and Antonius in a way that contrasts rather sharply with how he uses the same topic of family connections when attacking an individual of a rank superior to his own. Once again, Fulvia's former sister-in-law, Clodia, provides a useful comparison. In 56 BCE, Cicero defended his friend, M. Caelius Rufus, against charges of theft and poisoning brought against him by Clodia. A large part of Cicero's speech from that trial is dedicated to impugning her character. He depicts her as an overly and overtly libidinous widow; he repeatedly calls her a *meretrix* (courtesan), a rhetorical inversion of his assimilation in the Philippics of lower-class Fadia and Volumnia to proper wives. When he addresses the issue of Clodia's family, he presents her as a disappointment and a failed scion of a family of great antiquity and nobility, even taking on the persona of her famously stern and upright ancestor, Appius Claudius the Blind, as he upbraids her for her loose conduct. To return to the Philippics, Cicero uses much the same tactic against Antonius, whose family on

23. *Phil.* 3.15–17.
24. *Phil.* 2.90.

both sides had a long history of service to the state at the highest level. The sentiment is distilled to its most concise form in the conclusion of a later writer's version of Cicero's diatribe against Antonius: "Who indeed does not know that . . . he is fond of [his father-in-law] Bambalio, a man disparaged because of his nickname, and that he has treated his nearest relations just like I have been saying—as if he held some grudge against them because he had been born of so great a family?"[25]

A combination of high status and impeccable public behavior seems to have raised a woman above reproach: Antonius's mother and his first wife, his cousin Antonia, are treated rather differently from the other women in Antonius's life. Cicero throws at Antonius the scandalous accusation of adultery he had made against Antonia precisely on the point that Antonius had accused a woman of the utmost purity (*pudicissimam feminam*, Phil. 2.99).

Like Volumnia, Fulvia is woman with a dangerous, overt sexual power, but unlike Clodia, her sexuality is directed at only one man—or rather a series of men. In Cicero's telling, Fulvia is literally a *femme fatale*. In the Second Philippic, he blames her for the fact that she was widowed twice, asking Antonius: "And who has been found to attack my consulship? That is, except you and Publius Clodius, whose fate awaits you, just as it did Gaius Curio, since you keep that same lethal thing in your house." Elsewhere Fulvia is a woman "luckier for herself than she was for her husbands."[26] Cicero insinuates that Antonius took up with Fulvia while she was still married to Clodius,[27] and accuses him of having been so smitten with her as his wife that once, returning to Rome from Gaul, he snuck into the city after dark, disguised himself as a courier, and presented Fulvia with a letter professing his love and promising to give up his mistress.[28] This story paints Antonius as inappropriately dependent on Fulvia: Cicero calls him Fulvia's Catamite, a corruption of the name of the pretty young boy, Ganymede, who attracted Zeus's attention in Greek myth. The insult implies that Fulvia was the dominant sexual partner, a point Cicero hits again in the Sixth Philippic when he rails against the senate's assumption that Antonius will obey its command to desist from the siege at Mutina. With dripping sarcasm, he tells the assembled people of Rome, "Of course it will be

---

25. Cass. Dio 45.47.4.
26. *Phil.* 2.11 and 5.11.
27. *Phil.* 2.48.
28. *Phil.* 2.77 with 2.69–70.

easy for him, a man who has no control over himself, to obey this command to put himself under your control and that of the senators. What has he ever done of his own volition? He has always been pulled every which way by his lust, his frivolity, his madness, his drunkenness. There have always been two types of men who have held sway with him: pimps and bandits. He so delights in domestic debauchery and public murders that he more quickly obeyed a most rapacious woman than the senate and people of Rome."[29]

For Cicero, Fulvia is dangerous not only for Antonius, but also for Rome itself. He claims that she was inappropriately involved in the business of the state, especially her husband's illegal efforts to raise money by forging (for a fee) decrees in Caesar's name and taking bribes to arrange for grants of titles, kingdoms, and exemption from taxation. In the Third Philippic, Cicero claims that the gold Antonius had collected was weighed out in *quasilla*, baskets used by women to hold their wool-working. In the fifth speech in the series, he repeats the theme and goes one step further, claiming that Fulvia herself was auctioning provincial assignments and kingdoms to the highest bidder.[30] Perhaps there is some truth to this last claim, since in a much more private venue (a letter to Atticus, written just weeks after Caesar's assassination), Cicero implies that Fulvia was, already at that early date, involved in arranging a scheme to have a false decree issued that confirmed the Galatian king, Deiotarus, as the leader of his people. Cicero later claimed this arrangement cost Deiotarus ten million sesterces—an astronomical sum.[31]

Antonius and Octavian Unite

Cicero delivered the last Philippic in April 43, just after Antonius was finally defeated at Mutina. This caused political alignments to shift. Decimus, whose refusal to relinquish Gaul had drawn Antonius and his army to Mutina in the first place, had been killed while attempting to flee to Brutus in Macedonia. Hirtius and Pansa, consuls of the year who had worked alongside Octavian to raise Antonius's siege of the city, had succumbed to wounds they had sustained in the fighting. This

---

29. *Phil.* 6.4.
30. Cic., *Phil.* 3.10 and 5.11.
31. Cic., *Att.* 14.12.1 = SBA 366.1 with *Phil.* 2.95.

left Antonius and Octavian as the only two generals still in the field. The senate, fearing the dominance of either one of them, shored up the positions of the former conspirators by officially confirming Brutus and Cassius in their control of Macedonia and Syria and by giving Sextus Pompey, still based in Spain, control of the Roman fleet. Aware that cooperation in the face of senatorial opposition would benefit them all, Octavian, Antonius, and Lepidus (who had come to Antonius's aid late in the siege) formed a very uneasy alliance that would eventually be confirmed by law on November 27, 43, as an official Triumvirate (Board of Three Men) for Organizing the Republic.[32] At the urging of their troops (perhaps prompted by Antonius), the triumvirs confirmed their pact with the wedding of Octavian to Fulvia's daughter from her first marriage, Claudia. Thus Claudia, like Fulvia before her, was married off to shore up her stepfather's political alliance. The triumvirate was confirmed by a second union, or at least the promise of one. Lepidus's son had already been engaged to marry Antonius's daughter from his first marriage, named Antonia like her mother.[33] Because Antonia was only about seven years old in 43 BCE, the marriage—which would never come to be—had been put off indefinitely.

Once unified in their mission, the triumvirs exercised essentially unlimited and unchecked power over the state. One of their earliest actions was to institute proscriptions, a relatively efficient mechanism for removing political enemies and raising cash. Following the vicious example set by the dictator Sulla in the late 80s BCE, the triumvirs posted throughout the city a list of names of those who could be killed with impunity by anyone who came across them. The response to the postings was immediate. The city gates were shut, and all other routes out of Rome were cut off. The triumvirs ordered that all homes be thrown open to search. To ensure enthusiastic prosecution of the order, they offered rewards. A freeborn man who brought a victim's head to the triumvirs would be rewarded with a huge sum of money; a slave who brought in the head of his master would be granted his freedom, citizenship, and a smaller, but still substantial, sum.[34] The heads of the proscribed were displayed in the forum. One could tell when someone had been killed

---

32. The exact date is marked in the *Fasti Colotani* an ancient calendar; *Inscr. Ital.* 13.1, 273–4. See also App., *B Civ.* 4.2–3; Cass. Dio, 46.55.1–56.4; and Livy, *Per.* 120.
33. Cass. Dio 44.53.6 and 46.56.3.
34. App., *B Civ.* 4.7–11 includes a translation of the original declaration of the proscriptions.

in error (as often happens in such chaos): the corpse still had its head attached.

No one was safe. Lepidus proscribed his own brother, and Antonius put his mother's brother on the list. Both men had spoken against the triumvirs in the senate. Lepidus's brother managed to escape to Brutus in Macedonia, as did many of the proscribed. Others fled to Cassius in Syria and Sextus Pompey in Spain. Antonius's uncle was protected by Julia, who stormed into the Forum and told Antonius that his men could enter her house to kill her brother when they were ready to kill her, too. Antonius grudgingly lifted the order of proscription against his uncle, telling his mother that she was a good sister but a thoughtless mother.[35] He and Fulvia also protected a certain Sergius by hiding him in their home.[36] Far less fortunate was Cicero, whom Octavian, as a show of goodwill toward his new ally, Antonius, had added to the list. Years of hostility and the onslaught of the Philippics earned proscription for Rome's leading republican voice.

Some names were on the list to settle old scores, others to bring in money. The estates of the proscribed were forfeit, and now that Antonius, Lepidus, and Octavian had found common cause, war with Brutus and Cassius was imminent. The loyalty of the legions was expensive to maintain, and the state's finances were in shambles. Rome had lost an important stream of revenue when taxes stopped flowing in from Macedonia, Syria, and other eastern provinces where the conspirators were in control, and the conflict over Mutina had been costly. The demands of the soldiers were also driving the proscriptions forward in another, more sinister way. Appian reports that the troops, aware that the triumvirs depended on their goodwill for their own survival, were emboldened to demand particularly choice items from the estates of the proscribed or simply to kill some wealthy persons whose names were not on the list in order to obtain their property. To cover up the illegality, the triumvirs added names to the list after the fact.[37]

Not only men profited. Stories of women who made money in the triumvirs' proscriptions—and in the earlier round under Sulla—are not rare,[38] but Fulvia is alleged to have profited both personally and

35. App., *B Civ.* 4.37; Plut., *Vit. Ant* 20.
36. App., *B Civ.* 4.45.
37. App., *B Civ.* 4.35.
38. For example, Sulla's wife Metella: Plin., *HN* 36.116 (preserved in the context of Pliny's report of Curio's theater). On women profiting from Rome's civil wars, see Welch, "Memorable Women and Women in the Memory of Civil War," forthcoming.

financially from the proscriptions with exceptional rapacity and vindictiveness. Among the many whose names she reportedly added to the list was the owner of a particularly fine apartment building that she had long coveted. To save his life, the man simply handed it over to her. She took the property, but let the man be killed anyway. The murderers mistakenly brought his head to Antonius, who exclaimed that he had no idea who the man was and that they should take it to Fulvia. She then ordered that the head be displayed not in the Forum, along with the heads of the triumvirs' political victims, but at the building itself.[39] In the most gruesome account of Cicero's death, she is said to have toyed with his disembodied head. She pulled out his tongue, which had spoken so viciously against her in the senate, and pierced it with hairpins.[40] A more believable, and far more common, version of Cicero's death omits Fulvia altogether: Antonius ordered not only that Cicero's head be displayed in the Forum, but also the great orator's right hand because it had written against him so frequently.[41]

Fulvia Steps into the Fray

The proscriptions did not yield funds sufficient to their needs and desires, so the triumvirs also instituted numerous new taxes. One of the more innovative of these was a tax on the estates of the 1,400 wealthiest women in Rome. Although in times past women had willingly contributed their gold and jewelry to war efforts, this was a partisan move against the opposition. The women collectively decided to protest, but they could not properly address the triumvirs themselves and no man would take up their cause:[42] the risk of angering Antonius, Octavian, and Lepidus was too great. Thus the women opted to work through the channels available to them: they took their case to the female relatives of the triumvirs.[43] They received a positive reception from Antonius's mother and Octavian's sister, Octavia. They seem to have bypassed Claudia, wife of

---

39. App., *B Civ.* 4.29 and Cass. Dio 47.8.2–3.
40. Cass. Dio 47.8.3–5.
41. Other authors do not mention any involvement by Fulvia: Vell. Pat. 66.1–67.4; App., *B Civ.* 4.20; Plut., *Vit. Ant.* 20.2 and *Cic.* 48.1–6; Flor. 2.16.2.
42. Val. Max. 8.3.3.
43. App., *B Civ.* 4.32–4. Likewise, during the dictatorship of Sulla, people often sought to approach him by going to his wife Metella first (Plut., *Vit. Sull.* 6.12).

Octavian and daughter of Fulvia, altogether. Perhaps she was deemed too young or too much disdained by her husband to be influential.

The reception the women received from Fulvia was rather different: she refused to allow them to even enter her house. Appian, our main source for this episode, offers no explanation, leaving the impression that this was just another instance of Fulvia's vulgarity and arrogance. Other explanations are possible. Perhaps Fulvia was angered by the snubbing of Claudia, or maybe this was another instance of Fulvia's well-established allegiance to Antonius. Given her demonstrated political acumen, she probably also would have agreed that the triumvirs' financial situation merited such an extreme measure.[44] Another possibility is that Fulvia's ire was raised by the fact that women who had looked down on her for years for being only a second-tier aristocrat (recall Cicero's repeated insults about Fulvia's less-elevated status) or for being married to men of dubious moral status now came to ask for her help. When a delegation of some of the most prestigious women in the city, led by Hortensia, the daughter of a consul and descendent of a dictator, arrived at her door, Fulvia may have taken the opportunity to strike back at those at whose hands she had suffered.[45]

At Fulvia's rebuff, the delegation turned on its heel and stormed into the Forum, where the triumvirs were sitting at a tribunal. The crowd there, including soldiers, parted in order to let the women through. Hortensia then demonstrated that she had inherited her father's gift for dramatic and persuasive oratory by giving a speech so polished and powerful that people were still reading it 150 years later.[46] The triumvirs demanded that the women be removed from the Forum. As men moved to lead them away, however, the crowd became angry, pressing forward to protect Hortensia and her companions. At that point, the triumvirs, publicly chastened but not intimidated, announced that the issue was tabled until the next day, at which time a new notice was posted that the tax was now limited to only the 400 richest women in the city and that a new tax was levied on any man—citizen or foreigner—whose property was valued above a certain amount.

---

44. As proposed by Fischer 1999, 39–40.

45. Goldsworthy (2010, 232) suggests that Fulvia may have been thinking specifically about how these women offered no help to her earlier when Antonius was declared a public enemy.

46. Quint., *Inst.* 1.1.6. Unfortunately, it is now lost. Osgood (2006b, 540–2) has reservations about the details of Hortensia's great moment and suggests that her speech was, in fact, a later fabrication.

The year 42 BCE opened with Lepidus and Plancus, a man loyal to Antonius, as consuls. In the east, Brutus and Cassius controlled Macedonia and Syria and were officially confirmed in their command of those provinces by the senate. The situation was very unstable, and all sides prepared for war. Leaving Lepidus to maintain control of Italy, Octavian and Antonius headed for Macedonia in the hopes of engaging Brutus and Cassius on the battlefield. Their progress was delayed, however, by fleets commanded by Sextus Pompey and Staius Murcus, Brutus's and Cassius's admiral, that kept them bottled up in Italy.

Eventually Antonius and Octavian forced their way through the blockade and prepared their armies to face those of Brutus and Cassius at Philippi in Macedonia. The battle was the largest the Romans had ever seen up to that point: nineteen legions led by the triumvirs, seventeen by the conspirators. In the end, in April 42, Antonius emerged victorious. First Cassius and then Brutus died by suicide. Many of their supporters boarded ships and fled to Sextus Pompey for safety. Others sought clemency from Antonius, whose reputation as a great military man and the strongest of the triumvirs had been cemented by his victory. Octavian, as he was to do repeatedly later in life, missed the battlefield action due to illness and was nearly captured in his tent in the camp.[47] Sources disagree about what happened to Brutus's body. Some say that Antonius buried him at Philippi but sent his head back to his family at Rome, where Brutus's wife Porcia committed suicide. A version more charitable to Antonius says that he cremated the body and sent the ashes back to Brutus's mother, Servilia.[48]

Fulvia, Center Stage

With victory came complications, the most pressing of which were delivering the rewards that the triumvirs had promised to the men of twenty-eight demobilized legions and settling affairs in the east. The victors divided the tasks at hand between them.[49] Antonius was to stay in the east to raise money that had been promised to the troops and to

---

47. Cass. Dio, 47.45.2; Suet., *Aug.* 13.1. Octavian later wrote in his autobiography that he avoided capture because of a prophetic dream he had the night before (App., *B Civ.* 4.110).
48. Cass. Dio, 47.49.2; Suet., *Aug.* 13.1; Plut., *Vit. Ant.* 22.4; App., *B Civ.* 4.135. Servilia has now received her own extensive biography in Treggiari 2019.
49. App., *B Civ.* 5.10–13; Cass. Dio 48.1.2–2.4.

reconsolidate Rome's control of regions that had been good recruiting grounds for Brutus and Cassius. He would also become entangled in two romantic affairs, the first with a Cappadocian woman named Glaphyra and the second with Cleopatra, queen of Egypt. Octavian was to return to Italy in order to set about the unenviable job of settling the veterans, a less glamorous and very difficult task. To accomplish this, he had to remove the current residents of at least eighteen (but probably many, many more) preselected towns and turn over their estates, complete with equipment and slaves, to the soldiers who had been assigned to them.[50] A lot of people were going to be angry.

Octavian's progress home was delayed again by illness. When he finally arrived in Rome in early 41 BCE, the city was under control of his triumviral colleague, Lepidus, who had been in charge while Octavian and Antonius prosecuted the war. Despite his powerful position in the city, Lepidus is eclipsed in the ancient narratives by one of the consuls of the year, Antonius's surviving brother, Lucius, and his allies, including Fulvia, the equestrian Manius, and several commanders in the area who remained loyal to Antonius. In their accounts of the events that followed Octavian's return to the city, ancient authors probably overemphasize Fulvia's role and downplay Lucius's.

It is clear from events that Lucius was the leader of a powerful group that sought to protect Antonius's interests in Italy, but he is depicted as whinging and weak, dependent on Fulvia for whatever power he had. One writer, Cassius Dio, goes so far as to claim that, although Publius Servilius and Lucius Antonius were ostensibly the consuls of that year, in reality it was Lucius and Fulvia.[51] Dio goes on to claim that Fulvia was so powerful that she could disregard Lepidus, that the senate would not stand up to her, and that she could, merely on a whim, deny Lucius a triumph (an extravagant parade that a general could receive after a major victory, if the senate granted him one) that he claimed for an earlier victory over some Alpine tribes. Eventually, she capitulated and Lucius received his triumph, but Fulvia so outshone him on the day of the parade that the triumph appeared to be hers; Lucius was just there as her

---

50. The decision had been made and announced by the triumvirs in 43 (App., *B Civ.* 4.3; Cass. Dio 47.14.4–5 and 48.6.2–3) to ensure the loyalty of Caesar's veteran troops in the looming war with Brutus and Cassius. The literary and epigraphic evidence indicates that the confiscations were much more widespread than at first appears: at least forty towns were involved (Gabba 1971, 140).
51. Cass. Dio 48.4.1–6. In some modern accounts, Fulvia still bears the lion's share of the blame for the war with Octavian, e.g., Roller 2010, 84–5.

servant. There are many reasons to see such claims as exaggeration: Dio is one of the sources most hostile to Fulvia, and one should always be suspicious of self-contained episodes that have no effect on events (here, Fulvia denies Lucius his triumph but then he receives it anyway) and serve only to characterize prominent figures. The least believable element is, in fact, Fulvia's alleged usurpation of the senate's prerogative to grant a triumph. Yet, despite all the obvious inflation and distortion in this tale, it is clear that Fulvia was influential in the city, and she exercised a leadership role. In many ways, she was operating as did other aristocratic women tied to politically active men of the period, albeit in a much more public fashion.

As Octavian set about implementing the resettlement plan, tension in the city boiled over. Rage and unrest erupted on all sides. The displaced landowners flooded into Rome and, with support from the residents of the city, vigorously protested the loss of their property and the lack of any compensation.[52] On the other side, the soldiers were angered by what they perceived as foot-dragging by Octavian and, when he granted them land, they protested their assignments' meager size and undesirable locations. At one point, soldiers who had gathered before dawn to receive their allotments rioted because Octavian was late in arriving. A centurion who attempted to calm the crowd was killed by the mob; all Octavian could do to restore order was to ignore the murder and offer extra rewards to some who waited in the crowd.[53] The whole stressful situation was exacerbated by the ongoing menace of the navies of Sextus Pompey that controlled the waterways and cut off shipments of grain to Rome. The ensuing food shortage prompted a general strike.[54]

While the triumvirs will have anticipated the upset caused by the land redistribution, it probably came as a surprise to many that this was the issue that precipitated open hostility between Octavian and Antonius's allies in Rome. The plan had, after all, been devised in detail by Antonius, Lepidus, and Octavian together at the time they formed their alliance. It was already clear to everyone at the time that a war with Brutus and Cassius was on the horizon, and the triumvirs were looking for enticements to keep their troops loyal. The plan was then confirmed

---

52. Widespread sympathy for the displaced is echoed in poetry of the period: Verg., *Ecl.* 1 and 9; Prop., 1.21, 1.22, and 4.1.121–34; Hor., *Epist.* 2.2.41–54. Osgood's account of the *bellum Perusinum* (2006a, 108–201) interweaves the poetic material with prose historical accounts to powerful effect.
53. App., *B Civ.* 5.16.
54. App., *B Civ.* 5.18.

again after Philippi by Antonius himself when he agreed to the division of labor that kept him in the east and sent Octavian home to Italy. All this raises the question, then, as to what extent Lucius and his allies, including Fulvia, operated independently of Antonius in the events that unfolded next.

At first, Antonius's allies in Rome seem to have been doing exactly what they should to defend Antonius's interests. When Octavian attempted to exclude them from the settlement process, they accused him of trying to weaken the veterans' loyalty to Antonius by taking sole credit for the land allotments. Their efforts to hinder Octavian's progress and to insert themselves into the process only increased tension. Lucius went so far as to make a plea to the veterans themselves, bringing Fulvia and her sons by Antonius along with him to draw the sympathy of the men. Ultimately Octavian relented, agreeing that Lucius and the boys would accompany him as he set out to found some of the colonies. It is difficult to recover the details of what happened on that trip, but it resulted in Lucius accusing Octavian of having tried to kill him in an ambush—a claim Octavian denied. Despite extraordinary efforts by the senate and the soldiers themselves to smooth things over and to work out some kind of compromise, the situation continued to deteriorate. In a fit of anger, Octavian humiliated Fulvia by divorcing her daughter, Claudia. Although they had been married for two years, Octavian declared publicly that Claudia returned home with her virginity intact.[55]

The point of no return was Lucius's decision to take up the cause of the displaced landowners. It is not entirely clear what his motivation was: the landowners had been looking for some time for someone to champion them but had found no takers. It is possible that Lucius was looking for a base of supporters to counter Octavian's popularity, but Appian attributes Lucius's motivation to high-minded republicanism: he was eager to bring an end to the triumvirate and to restore the old Republic.[56] There were certainly men in the city who felt this way: it is known that some of Lucius's followers, among them Tisienus Gallus and Ti. Claudius Nero, the father of Rome's second emperor, had strong republican leanings. Such a position, however, would have put Lucius at odds with his older brother, who does not seem to have been interested

---

55. Cass. Dio 48.5.1–12.5; App., *B Civ.* 5.13–19; Plut., *Vit. Ant.* 20.1; Suet., *Aug.* 62.1. Welch 2012: 203–17.
56. App., *BC* 5.39 and 42–44, reinforced by 5.19 and 30.

in relinquishing his position as the first man in Rome.[57] It also requires the reader to ignore Appian's own earlier statements about Lucius's defense of his brother's interests in the initial round of land allotments.

Lucius's decision, whatever its motivation, caused a rift with Fulvia, who argued that her brother-in-law had chosen the wrong time to start a war.[58] This strongly suggests, but does not prove, that Lucius was not acting on orders from Antonius himself, a scenario that leaves Fulvia as the primary defender of Antonius's interests and perhaps explains Lucius's assertion that Fulvia favored monarchy, which Lucius associated with Antonius.[59] An alternative explanation is that Antonius tacitly approved of Lucius's actions and that Fulvia disagreed with them both. Either way, she was right that the timing was not to Lucius's advantage. Championing the landowners drew most of Italy to the Antonian cause, but it simultaneously undermined Antonius's position by alienating the veterans, whose loyalty he would need in the future.

Ultimately, Fulvia threw her support behind Lucius. It is impossible to determine with any certainty why she changed her mind. Appian reports that she only agreed after Manius persuaded her that a war would pull Antonius out of Cleopatra's arms and back to Italy and Fulvia, but this rings hollow. It smacks of hostility, making Fulvia out to be easily manipulated, and it is in line with other stories designed to paint her as petty and callous. More damning, however, is that it is also chronologically improbable, since Antonius had not yet taken up with Cleopatra.[60] Admittedly, by this point Fulvia will have heard stories of Antonius's dalliance with the Cappadocian woman named Glaphyra, whose son Antonius established on the throne there.[61] But it is difficult to believe that the woman who endured the presence of Volumnia in Rome would have been threatened by another competitor so far away.

---

57. Roddaz 1988, 340–3; Osgood 2006a, 160–1. Welch (2012, 220–1) argues that Antonius himself had an interest in (at least) appearing to defend the traditional *res publica*, so Lucius need not necessarily have chosen between his brother's interest and his republican ideals.

58. App., *B Civ.* 5.19.

59. In contrast to his own commitment to the Republic: App., *B Civ.* 5.54.

60. Welch 2012, 221. Roller, however, dates the beginning of Antonius's affair with Cleopatra several months earlier—to roughly the same time as the opening of hostilities between Octavian and Lucius (Roller 2010, 76). It is more likely, however, that Antonius took up with the queen of Egypt closer to the time of Lucius's surrender. See the following note.

61. App., *B Civ.* 5.7. That Antonius was entangled with Glaphyra in 41–40 is also strongly suggested by the fact that Octavian names her (and not Cleopatra), as an insult to Fulvia, in a poem he wrote right about the time of the *bellum Perusinum* (discussed later). For more on what is known about Glaphyra, see Roller 2018, 50–2.

It is also hard to reconcile the jilted wife who would start a war to bring her errant husband back to her with the woman who had enough political acumen to warn her brother-in-law away from picking the wrong time to provoke armed conflict.

But provoke he did: war broke out shortly after the attempted ambush. The conflict—called the Perusine War, *bellum Perusinum*, because the ancient city of Perusia (modern Perugia) was the focus of the action—would prove to be the last and greatest act of Fulvia's life. In some accounts, both ancient and modern, Fulvia bears the blame for inciting hostility against Octavian and/or prosecuting the war itself.[62] In other, more measured, more reliable versions, Fulvia maintains her leadership position among the Antonian faction and works to provide support for Lucius, who is clearly at the helm of the military operation.

After the failed ambush and unsuccessful efforts to repair the rift between Octavian and Lucius, brokered by their soldiers and by the senate,[63] there was nothing left but to fight it out. Octavian remained north of Rome. Lucius withdrew with his supporters to Praeneste (modern Palestrina), a city twenty-three miles south of the capital. Fulvia left Rome to seek refuge with Lepidus, although it is not clear where he was.[64] It is possible that he, too, was with Lucius at Praeneste, along with many senators and equestrians sympathetic to their cause. If so, perhaps Fulvia tarried in Rome for a time before heading south: she does not seem to have been at Praeneste for a meeting with a senatorial delegation that was a last-ditch effort to negotiate a truce.[65]

Wherever Fulvia was, she did not sit idly by. Later in the winter, Lucius found himself caught between two armies loyal to Octavian— one of them led by the young Agrippa, who would quickly prove himself to be the greatest general of his generation—and withdrew to the fortified Umbrian city of Perusia. Octavian's generals, eventually joined by Octavian himself, pursued Lucius and settled in for the siege. As the situation in the city became increasingly desperate, Fulvia wrote to commanders loyal to Antonius, urging them to come to Lucius's aid.[66]

---

62. Livy, *Per.* 125–6; Vell. Pat. 2.74; Bauman 1992, 86–9.
63. Where Dio has Octavian seek to negotiate with Lucius and Fulvia (48.10.2–3), Appian has the soldiers themselves repeatedly attempt to negotiate between Octavian and Lucius (see also 5.21–3). Appian puts much of the blame for failed negotiations on Manius (5.22), as does his Antonius at the conclusion of the episode (5.52 and 66).
64. App., *B Civ.* 5.21 with commentary of Gabba 1970, *ad loc.* Delia (1991, 203) thinks he is at Praeneste with the senators and equestrians who decamped there.
65. App., *B Civ.* 5.29.
66. App., *B Civ.* 5.33.

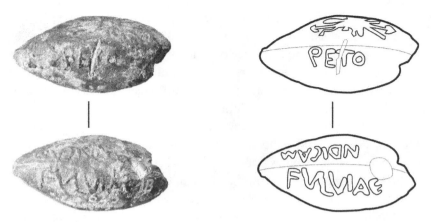

FIGURE 4.1. Sling bullet with an insult for Fulvia.
Source: L. Benedetti and S. Olmos.

Ventidius and Pollio left Gaul and moved toward Perusia, getting so close that the besieged troops could see signal fires set in their allies' camps. But Ventidius and Pollio could, or perhaps would, come no closer; the siege remained in place. It is perhaps at this time that Fulvia was also in contact with Sextius, Antonius's ally who served as governor of the province of Africa.[67] Fulvia then raised additional troops herself and dispatched them to Perusia under the command of Plancus. On route, they destroyed a legion loyal to Octavian that had been on its way to Rome, but Plancus and his men were blocked from reaching their goal. Lucius and his forces held out through much of the winter, but as starvation set in, they surrendered early in the spring of 40 BCE.

Fulvia's efforts on Lucius's behalf lie at the root of hostile claims that she strapped on a sword and addressed the troops at Praeneste, that she had taken the city by storm, and that she fomented mutiny among Octavian's soldiers.[68] This image of Fulvia as a woman who transgressed the confines of the proper aristocratic matronal behavior has been reinforced, for modern scholars, by a rather spectacular collection of sling bullets from the siege of Perusia (Figure 4.1).[69]

67. Cass. Dio, 48.22.3.
68. Cass. Dio, 48.10.3–4; Livy, *Per.* 125; Vell. Pat. 2.74.
69. Rihil 2009 is a good introduction to *glandes* as a class of objects and the difficulties they pose for researchers. Zangemeister's collection of inscribed lead bullets (1885) is a useful place to start for any study on the topic in a Roman context, but the field has developed dramatically in sophistication and scope in the more than a century since its publication. Benedetti 2012 offers the most comprehensive collection of Perusine bullets.

Fulvia's Final Act   97

Roman sling bullets are lead pellets about two inches in length. They were hurled by skilled slingers using a leather strap, and they are certainly heavy enough to cause serious injury on impact. They sometimes bear messages, most often advertising the military units who used them or their commanders and other officers. At Perusia, the largest group of inscribed bullets announce "Commander Caesar" (Octavian preferred to remind everyone that he, now, was Caesar) as well as the names of legions, officers, and generals working under Octavian's command:[70] one ancient writer singles out Octavian's slingers as being exceptionally skilled.[71] Three bullets bearing the inscription *Felix / Caesar imp(erator)* (Lucky Caesar the Commander) engage in a bit of propagandizing.[72]

Octavian's opponents lobbed missiles bearing the name of Fulvia's husband, rather than that of Lucius.[73] This is perhaps a sign that Lucius's troops were forced to scrounge for supplies and use whatever was close to hand, or perhaps it is an indication that Lucius worked to remind his own troops and Octavian that he was, as least ostensibly, fighting on his brother's behalf, or that the soldiers thought of themselves as Antonius's men.[74] These interpretations are, of course, not mutually exclusive.

A more interesting category of messages are the taunts and boasts written on the bullets, akin to the message "With love, from Manchester" written by Royal Air Force airmen on a bomb intended for ISIS in 2017 after the suicide bombing at a rock concert in that city.[75] Taunts and

70. Benedetti 2012, n. 3–28, 37–43. Other officers named include the general Q. Salvidienus Rufus Salvius, one *tribunus militum*, and several *primipili*.
71. App., *B Civ.* 5.33.
72. Benedetti 2012, n. 26–8.
73. Benedetti 2012, n. 1–2.
74. This last option, proposed by Livadiotti 2013, 86, is the least attractive because Antonius's name was clearly part of the original mold used to make the bullets: the soldiers in the field are unlikely to have been part of the decision to label the *glandes* in this way.
75. Images of labeled bombs can be found at https://www.news18.com/news/world/uks-royal-air-forcecrew-write-love-from-manchester-on-bomb-for-isis-report-1414953.html, https://metro.co.uk/2015/11/16/photosof-us-hellfire-missiles-scrawled-with-from-paris-with-love-are-probably-fakes-5505789/, and http://www.thedrive.com/the-war-zone/12623/message-on-bunker-buster-bomb-scolds-isis-for-making-me-miss-game-of-thrones (all accessed August 19, 2018). The phenomenon has a long tradition. See, for example, the explanation offered by J. Corbett, in his memoir of the siege at Khe Sanh during the Vietnam War (2003, 144), "We write messages to the enemy on the stabilizer fins of some of our mortar rounds before we fire them. The best place to write a message is on the tail fins, because they are the only part of the mortar round left intact after it explodes. We know that the enemy will get the message. Most of the messages we write are simple and to the point, such as 'Fuck you.' We write things that would never appear on a Hallmark greeting card. Occasionally, we get personal and write something nasty about the enemy's mother. Writing these messages is something to do, and it gives us a laugh. Soldiers in World War II wrote on bombs. Bombs dropped in the European theater usually had a written derogatory remark about

threats on the Perusine bullets are directed at both sides of the conflict, such as "Hey, Octavian, you suck!" and "Lucius Antonius, baldy, you're dead. Victory belongs to Gaius Caesar!"[76] A surprisingly large number of them bear sexually explicit statements, something very unusual for collections of bullets from other battles in the Roman Republic.[77] Sometimes the bullets "talk" in the first person: "I'm looking for Octavian's ass."[78] Fulvia appears on a talking bullet that claims "I'm looking for Fulvia's clitoris" (Figure 4.1).[79] Another bears her name and an unintelligible second word.[80] A third (now lost) bore the message "L. Antonius, baldy, and Fulvia, spread your cheeks!"[81]

The bullets imply that Fulvia was at Perugia, but this seems to be incorrect. The last place we can securely locate her is Praeneste, 125 miles away. This raises the questions, who put her name on the bullets, and why? It is tempting to attribute such coarse statements to soldiers entertaining themselves on the eve of battle. Lead is a soft metal, and it is easy to carve letters into it. Yet almost all of these scurrilous messages are, like the names of legions and commanders on other bullets, in relief: they were part of the mold used to form the bullets at the workshop that produced them en masse. Someone made an executive decision to include them. Unfortunately, it is impossible to say how far up the chain of command that individual was.

Did Octavian himself order the insults? It is certainly possible. It would have been a valuable piece of public relations to have his men believe that they were fighting troops led by a woman (what could be less threatening?) and, simultaneously, to demean his opponents by claiming they took orders from one. Furthermore, the sexual tone of the bullets'

Hitler. Bombs dropped in the Pacific theater usually had a derogatory remark about the Japanese emperor. Vietnam is our war, and we do as we please. We have our own vocabulary."

76. Benedetti 2012, n. 30 and 33. He is always named Octavian on bullets bearing insults.

77. Noted by Hallett 1977, 154.

78. Benedetti 2012, n. 31. Hallett understands this bullet as calling Octavian "Octavia" (Hallett 2015, 250).

79. Hallett 1977, 154–60. When I inspected this bullet at the Museo Archeologico Nazionale dell'Umbria in Perugia in July 2017, I was only able to read [.]e[.]o / [. .]vdica[.] / Fulvia[.]. The sad state of the text is confirmed by Benedetti's photograph (n. 32), although he reports a robust reading of Peto / [l]andicam / Fulviae. Benedetti's reading is slightly less conjectural than that in Zangemeister 1885, 55, n. 56.

80. Benedetti 2012, n. 32 and 60. The latter reads Fulvna / ul[.]r[--].

81. The antiquarian Lovatti, in writing to the item's owner, Guardabassi, in 1862, refers to the bullet as a "guazzabuglio," a real mess (letter presented in Benedetti 2012, 108 n. 4). Lovatti then lost the item sometime before Zangemeister published his volume in 1885 (n. 65 in his catalogue). Zangemeister thought the piece was legitimate, but it is not clear that he saw it himself.

message was not too coarse for Octavian. In fact, they are very much in line with a short poem he wrote at about the same time as the battle at Perugia. I have retained the coarse character of the original Latin:[82]

> Because Antonius fucked Glaphyra, Fulvia decided that this should be *my* punishment, that I should fuck her. That *I* should fuck *her*? What if Manius begged me to fuck him up the ass? Would I do it? I don't think so, if I were wise. "Fuck or let's fight," she says. But don't you know my cock is dearer to me than my life? Let the war trumpets sound!

In sum, if it was not Octavian himself who ordered those messages to be added to the bullets, it will have been one of his subordinates who thought it would delight him.

Her behavior in the Perusine War shows Fulvia as we have seen her before: a vigorous defender of her husband's interests and a woman with real political acumen. Throughout the winter of 41–40, Fulvia consistently acted in coordination with her husband's most powerful allies—as she and her mother-in-law, Julia, had done earlier in 43, when they proved instrumental in rallying senatorial support for Antonius in the face of Cicero's vigorous efforts to persuade that body to declare him a public enemy. This is very much in line, albeit in a more public fashion, with what we know about the activities of other prominent women of this same period, such as Terentia, the wife of Cicero, and the unknown woman commonly called "Turia," whose story is preserved in an inscription that once adorned her tomb. Both of these women defended their menfolk's property and worked alongside their friends and supporters to lobby for their recall from exile.[83]

Fulvia also demonstrated remarkable independence and initiative, drawing on her own social network to advance Antonius's interests. Given his political standing as the most powerful man in Rome, it is not surprising that Fulvia's efforts on his behalf brought her into contact with other members of Rome's political elite. Of course she had access to leading equestrians and senators and, as the situation in Rome

---

82. Preserved in Martial 11.20. Hallett 1977, 161, and 2015, 248. Hallett also points out that several bullets (Benedetti 2012, n. 29–31 and perhaps also 34) with messages portraying Octavian as the recipient of anal and oral penetration, a disgraceful thing for an aristocratic Roman man, echo what ancient sources tell us his enemies said about him.

83. On Terentia, see n. 17. For Terentia and "Turia," who was not yet married to the man whose property and aged mother she protected while he fled Rome, see Osgood 2014, 30–9.

became untenable, it is reasonable that she sought refuge with Lepidus out of concern for her own and her children's safety.[84] It is also reasonable to think that she knew Ventitdius, Pollio, and the other Antonian commanders on a personal level, so her letters encouraging them to come to Lucius's aid at Perusia may not have seemed presumptuous.

Fulvia's overt political activity can be set in the context of the activities of other women with ties to the most important players of the late 40s BCE. Porcia, daughter of Cato and wife of Brutus, was privy to the planning of Caesar's assassination and took part (along with her sister-in-law, Tertulla) in the huddle of republicans at Antium in June of 44. Servilia, Porcia's mother-in-law, was there, too, as was Cicero. He reports that Servilia told the others she would set about getting the senate to retract Brutus's assignment to the grain commission, presumably by calling in some favors from individual senators who were in her debt for one reason or another.[85] Julia, Antonius's mother, protected her brother from the proscriptions and later played a role in negotiating an alliance between Antonius and Sextus Pompey.[86] Mucia, mother of Sextus Pompey, and Scribonia, his wife, helped negotiate, in 39 BCE, the treaty of Misenum between him and the triumvirs.[87] All of these women worked alongside and offered valuable counsel to the men doing the fighting. Fulvia stands out as the most visible: whereas most of them worked quietly behind the scene, Fulvia's activities in the military camps in the lead up to the Perusine War and, especially, in the recruitment of troops to relieve the siege of Perusia—an act requiring initiative, independence, and persistence—were visible to all. But even the recruitment of troops has a comparandum in Octavia's presentation of Antonius with military supplies and soldiers later in 35 (see p. 116). But whereas Fulvia's aid is generally interpreted as an egregious transgression of matronal norms, Octavia's gift is a sign of her unwavering devotion to her husband. The difference lays bare how the hostility of our sources about Fulvia have shaped our picture of her.[88]

Fulvia's importance to the Antonian cause, and to Antonius himself, is made clear by the aftermath of Lucius's surrender at Perusia. While

---

84. App., *B Civ.* 5.21 with Delia 1991, 203–5, and Kaden 2012, 97–9.
85. Cic., *Att.* 15.11.1–2 = *SBA* 389.1–2; Plut., *Vit. Brut.* 13.1–11; Treggiari 2019, 188–96.
86. App., *B Civ.* 5.52; Cass. Dio, 48.15.2; Plut., *Vit. Ant.* 32.1.
87. App., *B Civ.* 5.69 and 72 (where Scribonia is erroneously named Julia).
88. Plut., *Vit. Ant.* 53.2; App. *B Civ.* 5.138. This parallel was pointed out to me by Miranda Chambers.

some of Lucius's more prominent followers escaped to Sextus Pompey, Antonius, or Antonius's allies,[89] Octavian slaughtered many others. The majority of the citizens of Perusia paid with their lives for harboring the Antonian forces, and the city was burned to the ground. Octavian's behavior was so brutal that some said he had sacrificed 300 men at an altar to his now-divine adoptive father, Julius Caesar.[90] Our sources do not credit the story, but it was still a prevalent enough part of the tradition that Suetonius and Dio felt the need to report it.

All this makes the gentle treatment of the leaders of the Antonian cause even more shocking. Octavian clearly recognized that he still needed Antonius's goodwill. Lucius was sent to Spain as a legate, ostensibly to oversee the two governors of provinces there. More likely this was so that Octavian could claim to have honored Lucius's rank and so that the two governors could keep an eye on Lucius. This is the last we ever hear of him: it is likely that he died while on this assignment. The fact that he did not flee to Antonius for protection is perhaps evidence of his independence from his brother's interests, but it cannot be proved. The other Antonian generals, Munatius Plancus, Ventidius, and Asinius Pollio, seemed to have suffered no ill effects: they all continued to be active on the battlefield and in politics for the rest of their lives. Fulvia and the children were permitted to leave Italy, but they did not sneak away in the middle of the night. The Antonian generals made sure Fulvia was accompanied by a massive military escort of 3,000 cavalry as she and her children made their way to Brundisium, where an escort of five ships awaited them.[91]

The Last Scene

Fulvia and Antonius reunited in Athens, Greece. They were eventually joined by his mother, Julia. Antonius is said to have blamed Fulvia, Lucius, and especially their ally, Manius, for the war with Octavian. Yet because Antonius's role in the whole affair is not clear, it is difficult to know if that is back-casting from his reconciliation with Octavian later that year, when Antonius needed to sidestep any responsibility for

---

89. App., *B Civ.* 5.50.
90. Cass. Dio, 48.14.3–6, and Suet., *Aug.* 15.1.
91. Cass. Dio, 48.15.1; App., *B Civ.* 5.50.

the Perusine War.⁹² Antonius seems to have decided to proceed with caution, concealing his plans. Julia had come from Sextus Pompey, to whom she had fled when the situation in Italy became too dangerous. She arrived in Greece accompanied by envoys and bearing a proposal for an alliance with Pompey against Octavian. Antonius hedged. In one account, he replied that he might take up the offer if he could not effect an alliance with both Pompey and Octavian; in another, he is said to have made peace with Octavian while secretly committing to an alliance with Pompey against him.⁹³ Either way, Antonius delayed the return home of a delegation of veterans that had come to him seeking aid, keeping them in suspense as to what he would do.

At some point shortly after arriving in Greece, Fulvia moved to the city of Sicyon, near Corinth. Antonius departed to deal with Octavian in Italy. While he was away, she took ill and died. To her last breath, the sources portray her as petty and vindictive. Dio says that she was angry that Antonius had left her when she was unwell and made her illness worse to spite him. Appian makes her out to be weak, saying she was heartbroken that Antonius was angry with her and because of his torrid affair with Cleopatra, which was indeed an issue by the spring of that year. Dio, Appian, and Plutarch agree that both Antonius and Octavian were relieved when Fulvia died: she was a convenient scapegoat for the Perusine War. The truth, whatever it is, cannot be recovered.⁹⁴

---

92. App., *B Civ.* 5.52; Cass. Dio, 48.15.2 and 48.27.4.
93. Compare App., *B Civ.* 5.52 with Cass. Dio 48.29.1–2.
94. Cass. Dio 48.28.3; App., *B Civ.* 5.59; Plut., *Vit. Ant.* 30.2–4.

5

After Fulvia's Death

The struggle for preeminence at Rome barely paused to mark Fulvia's death: it looked as if another round of civil war might follow on the heels of Octavian's victory over Lucius at Perusia. Now, of the three triumvirs, only two were still in competition. Lepidus, who had been increasingly irrelevant since the deaths of Brutus and Cassius, does not figure prominently in the sources after his departure for North Africa in 40 BCE. It was clear to all that the next round of fighting would be a contest between Octavian in the west and Antonius in the east. Each now sought to strengthen his position by cultivating Sextus Pompey, then in control of Spain and Sicily. In the aftermath of the fall of Perusia, Antonius's mother, Julia, had arrived in Greece with an offer of an alliance from Sextus. Antonius was receptive but apparently not fully committed. Even so, Sextus's fleet renewed its attacks on the Italian coast on Antonius's behalf. Octavian, now free of Fulvia's daughter, Claudia, married Scribonia, who shared a name with her niece who was Sextus's wife. For his part, Sextus seems to have been, wisely, unimpressed by this demonstration of allegiance.[1] The union, and the alliance, would not last long.

A New Marriage and an Old Affair

The escalating hostility between Antonius and Octavian came to a head in the port town of Brundisium on Italy's southeastern coast in the fall of 40 BCE, a few months after Fulvia's death. Antonius sailed toward Italy

---

1. App., *B Civ.* 5.53 with Osgood 2006a, 187–93 and Welch 2012, 230–8.

with a fleet, only to be blocked from entering Brundisium by the local residents and a garrison of troops that Octavian had supplied to the city. Antonius responded with a blockade, and Brundisium appealed to Octavian for assistance. Soon after, he arrived with reinforcements.

In the lull before the fighting began, the soldiers in the two camps began to talk with one another. There was a groundswell of support for a negotiated settlement; the rank-and-file had no interest in fighting any longer. The result was the Peace of Brundisium. It confirmed Antonius in the east; Lepidus was given the province of Africa; and Octavian had control of Italy and the west, with a provision that he could start a war with Sextus so long as no other arrangement with him had been reached. As happened the last time their soldiers forced Octavian and Antonius to agree to work together (in 43 when they first formed their alliance with Lepidus), their renewed friendship was reinforced by new familial arrangements. This time, the widower Antonius married Octavian's recently widowed sister, Octavia. Her husband, Marcellus, had died so recently, in fact, that the senate had to be asked to release Octavia from the required ten-month mourning period.[2] Not surprisingly, the senators consented.

The new marriage was destined to last just as long as the renewed alliance between Octavian and Antonius. At first, Antonius's relationship with Octavia—and his relationship with her brother—went well. For most of the period between the fall of 40 and spring of 37, Antonius and Octavia lived together, briefly in Rome and then in Athens, when Antonius took possession of the provinces guaranteed him by the Peace of Brundisium. Married life, once again, seems to have agreed with Antonius. Octavia is reported to have been a woman of exceptional beauty, charm, and refinement, a paragon of matronal virtue who tempered the impulsive Antonius, much as Fulvia had done before.[3] Their household included not only the three young sons that Fulvia had left behind[4]—Curio, Antyllus, and Iullus—but also Octavia's son and two daughters by Marcellus, her first husband. To this expansive brood were soon added another two new daughters, both named—like their older half-sister—Antonia.[5] Out of sight, but probably not out of Octavia's mind, were two other children, twins born to Cleopatra, queen of Egypt,

---

2. Livy, *Per.* 127; Plut., *Vit. Ant.* 31.1–3; App., *B Civ.* 5.64; Cass. Dio, 48.31.3.
3. App., *B Civ.* 5.76.
4. On the fates of Fulvia's two oldest children, Claudia and Claudius, see pp. 110–111.
5. Plut., *Vit. Ant.* 35.1 and 87.3.

late in 40—the result of the affair between Cleopatra and Antonius that seems to have started up sometime around the fall of Perusia.

In the spring of 37, after two years in Greece, Antonius and his family returned to Italy. His relationship with Octavian, never easy, had been deteriorating, and the triumvirate, originally approved by the senate for a five-year period, had technically expired on the preceding January 1. It was time to renew their compact. In addition, Antonius brought Octavian desperately needed military aid to help in the ongoing war against Sextus Pompey. Octavia arranged a meeting between her husband and her brother at the coastal city of Tarentum, at which it was agreed that the triumvirate would be renewed until the end of 33. Once again, the political alliance was strengthened by a marital arrangement. Antyllus, Antonius and Fulvia's teenaged son, was engaged to Octavian's two-year-old daughter, Julia.[6]

Antonius, accompanied by Antyllus and his stepson, Curio, then returned to the east to take up Caesar's long-delayed war against the Parthians. Octavia and the younger children stayed in Italy. Husband and wife would not see each other again. Once he reached the city of Antioch (modern Antakya, Turkey), Antonius summoned Cleopatra to meet him there. She brought with her the twins, named Alexander Helios and Cleopatra Selene, whom Antonius had not yet met. He acknowledged them as his own—a humiliating development for Octavia, but an advantageous one for her brother. Octavian, always eager to undermine Antonius's popularity in Italy, used this episode to paint his rival as corrupt, decadent, and beholden to a foreign temptress.[7]

Eventually, Cleopatra (perhaps already pregnant with another son, to be named Ptolemy Philadelphus) and the twins returned to Alexandria, and Antonius took up his campaign against the Parthians. It did not go well: he suffered resounding losses in Parthian territory in 36–35. Octavian saw an opportunity to force Antonius's hand and sent Octavia to Greece with reinforcements, a gift to Antonius from his wife and his brother-in-law.[8] To accept them would mean submission; to reject them would be an unforgivable insult. Antonius, who had gone to Alexandria after the Parthian disaster, split the difference. He sent word to Octavia that she should return to Italy immediately, but she should

---

6. Julia was the daughter of Octavian's second wife, Scribonia, whom he divorced on the day she gave birth. Cass. Dio 48.34.3, 48.54.4, 51.15.5.
7. Plut., *Vit. Ant.* 36.3; Suet., *Aug.* 17.1; Cass. Dio 49.32.4–5.
8. Plut., *Vit. Ant.*, 53.1–54.2; Cass. Dio 49.33.3–4 and 50.3.2.

leave the forces and supplies she had brought with her in Greece. He also divorced her. Octavian had his pretext for war.

Antonius Meets His End

It would take another four years to reach the final conflict, a sea battle off the Greek coast at a place called Actium, where Octavian's forces routed the combined fleets of Antonius and his many allies, including Cleopatra and Herod, the king of Judea. Herod, along with many of the other eastern kings who had signed on for the war, defected to Octavian after the defeat. Antonius's nineteen legions negotiated a surrender to Octavian. Antonius, Cleopatra, and the remnants of their forces retreated to Alexandria, where eventually Octavian pursued them.[9]

Despite repeated embassies to Octavian from Antonius and Cleopatra, there was no negotiating their way out of the present circumstance. The invasion of Alexandria came in August, 30 BCE. The events that followed, told at great length by Plutarch and Dio and immortalized in Shakespeare's *Antony and Cleopatra*, are the stuff of high drama.[10] Antonius prepared to defend the city. He was successful at first, but soon his fleet and his cavalry defected to Octavian. Cleopatra, hearing that Antonius believed she had betrayed him, sought refuge in the massive tomb that she had, following the practice of her ancestors, built for herself. Antonius heard that she was dead and decided to join her by suicide. He stabbed himself with a sword, only to learn at almost the last minute that she was still alive. He ordered his attendants to take him to her at her tomb. He died in her arms.

Cleopatra committed suicide, too. The story is that after she was taken captive by Octavian, she was desperate to avoid the humiliation of being displayed in Octavian's triumphal parade when he returned to Rome. One of her servants snuck past the guards and into her cell with a basket containing an asp. She held it to her breast, so that she might die by its poisonous bite. Octavian's efforts to keep her alive—he longed to parade her before the Roman people—were for nought.[11]

---

9. Ancient accounts of the battle are numerous, including Plut., *Vit. Ant.* 60.1–68.5 and Cass. Dio 50.11.1–50.35.6. For a consideration of poetic treatments by Horace, Vergil, and Propertius, see Gurval 1995, 137–278.
10. Plut., *Vit. Ant.* 74.1–86.4; Cass. Dio 51.5.1–51.15.4.
11. For justified skepticism about the details of Cleopatra's suicide, see Roller 2010, 147–9.

Octavian was nothing if not thorough. The immediate threat to his preeminence was gone, but the children whom Antonius and Cleopatra had left behind might prove to be a rallying point for those who opposed him. He saw to it that Fulvia's two sons, the young Curio and Antyllus, who were in Alexandria, were put to death. Of Curio's death, no details are preserved.[12] Antyllus was betrayed by his tutor and killed at an altar of the Divine Julius Caesar. The tutor then stole a piece of jewelry from Antyllus's beheaded corpse; Octavian had the man crucified for the theft.[13] Cleopatra's son by Julius Caesar, Caesarion, had escaped the city and, in one version, was killed en route to Ethiopia; in another version of the story, he was persuaded to return to Alexandria, where he was quickly dispatched by Octavian. Octavian is said to have hesitated to sign Caesarion's death warrant—he was, after all, Octavian's adoptive half-brother.[14] But ultimately there could be only one son of Caesar.

Cleopatra's other children, the twins and Ptolemy, who were at that time aged 11 and 7, were sent to live with long-suffering Octavia. This was a highly unusual move that surely attracted attention in Italy. Death or exile were the expected fates of children in their position.[15] It is likely that the youngest, Ptolemy, died either en route or shortly after his arrival in Rome. He did not appear in Octavian's triumph the next year. Alexander Helios and Cleopatra Selene were displayed in the parade, however, dressed as the Sun (Helios) and the Moon (Selene), alongside an effigy of their mother, who was depicted complete with an asp.[16]

The triumph is the last time we hear of Alexander Helios, so it is possible that he, too, died not long after the triumph.[17] Cleopatra Selene, the sole survivor of Cleopatra's children, lived into adulthood.[18] Some years after her arrival in Octavia's household, she was married to Octavia's ward, Juba II, who had been brought to Rome as a captive after the death of his father, King Juba I of Numidia, who had fought for Pompey and the Republican cause in the war with Caesar in the early 40s and whose cavalry had been responsible for the death of Fulvia's second husband, Curio.

12. Cass. Dio 51.2.5.
13. Plut., *Vit. Ant.* 81.1; Suet., *Aug.* 17.5; Cass. Dio 51.6.1–2 and 51.15.5.
14. Plut., *Vit. Ant.* 81.2–82.1; Cass. Dio 51.6.1–2.
15. Harders 2009, 223.
16. Plut., *Vit. Ant.* 86.3; Cass. Dio 51.21.8.
17. Roller 2018, 31. For an argument that Alexander may have lived to adulthood, see Harders 2009, 236–7.
18. The most extensive treatments of Cleopatra Selene are Roller 2003, 76–90, and 2018, 27–48.

FIGURE 5.1. The Royal Mausoleum of Mauretania in Algeria.
Source: Dave G. Houser / Alamy Stock Photo.

The newlyweds were installed as monarchs in the client kingdom of Mauretania in northwest Africa, where they turned the city of Iol, newly renamed Caesarea (now Chercel, Algeria), into an impressive capital.[19] Cleopatra Selene disappears from the record after the birth of her son somewhere between 13 and 9 BCE. She named him Ptolemy—a daring and dramatic announcement that she saw herself as the heir to the Ptolemaic Empire. Her eulogy, written by the poet Crinagoras of Mytilene, survives.[20] She and her husband, who outlived her by some decades, were probably buried in a joint tomb now known as the Royal Mausoleum of Mauretania.[21] Its impressive remains can still be seen today (Figure 5.1).

Upon his return to Rome, Octavian strove to ensure that the memory of Antonius was obliterated. Many of the monuments in the city that celebrated him were removed; others were allowed to remain, but his name was chiseled off. His property was confiscated by the government,

---

19. See especially Roller 2003, 119–62.

20. On his relationship with Cleopatra Selene, see Roller 2003, 87–9. A collection of Crinagoras's poetry, including Cleopatra Selene's eulogy and another poem commemorating her marriage to Juba II, is available in Greek with English translation and extensive commentary in Ypsilanti 2018, n. 18 and 25, respectively.

21. Roller 2003, 128–30.

although his two daughters by Octavia were permitted to inherit part of the estate.[22] The senate forbade that any member of the clan be named Marcus, and the day of his birth was declared ill-omened.[23] This last indignity has given rise to one of Roman history's more humorous ironies: it is precisely because Octavian tried to erase the memory of Antonius's birthdate that we know he was born on January 14. An ancient calendar, found in the Italian town of Veroli and dated to the reign of Augustus's successor, the emperor Tiberius, notes on that date: "The day is split in half [i.e., business could be conducted in the morning, but not in the afternoon]. It was declared unpropitious by a decree of the senate [because it was] Antonius's birthday."[24]

Fulvia's Progeny

Despite the violence visited upon Curio, Antyllus, and Caesarion, Octavian was relatively gentle with the rest of Fulvia's and Cleopatra's children, as we have already seen in the case of Cleopatra Selene. Indeed, the sources stress that Octavian, soon to become the emperor Augustus, took pride in the caring (or, at least, benign) relationships he maintained with Claudius, Iullus, and their half-sisters, the Antonias. These relationships may have been based on genuine affection, but one cannot ignore the value of such connections for strengthening Augustus's public image as a man of loyalty, clemency, and compassion.[25]

The fates of Fulvia's remaining children varied. Her only daughter, Claudia, drops out of the historical record after her shameful divorce by Octavian in 41.[26] She may well have died not long after that; it is likely the sources would report if she had married again. Her brother, Claudius, already an adult at the time of his mother's death, may well be considered the most successful of Fulvia's progeny. When he was still quite young, his stepfather praised him in a letter to Cicero as showing promise.[27]

---

22. Cass. Dio 51.15.7. It is through the two Antonias that Antonius's bloodline became part of the Roman imperial household. Antonia Minor was the mother of the future emperor Claudius and grandmother of Caligula; her older sister was the grandmother of the emperor Nero.
23. Cass. Dio 51.19.3–5; Plut., *Vit. Cic.* 49.6 and *Vit. Ant.* 86.5.
24. Degrassi 1963, 158–9.
25. Harders 2009.
26. See p. 94.
27. Cic., *Att.* 14.13A.2–3 = *SBA* 367A.2–3, with commentary. Note that Antonius refers to him as Claudius. In his response (*Att.* 14.13B.4–5 = 367B.4–5), Cicero calls him Clodius.

Later in life, Claudius's reputation was less positive: he is described as a wastrel with a penchant for decadent living and a shameful attachment to a prostitute.[28] Even so, he reached high political office (the praetorship) at some point after Antonius's death, and he was an augur, one of Rome's prestigious public priesthoods. Claudius's two children, Fulvia's grandchildren, survived to adulthood and maintained the family's stature in the early empire. His son went on to become consul in either 21 or 22 CE, and his daughter married P. Quinctilius Varus, who served as consul in 13 BCE but who is far more famous for having lost his life and the lives of several legions in an ambush by German tribes in the Teutoburg Forest in 9 CE. Claudia was later prosecuted for adultery.[29]

The highlights of Claudius's own successful political career are recorded on his funeral vase (Figure 5.2), found in Rome and now in the Louvre Museum in Paris. The vase bears his full name as an advertisement of his distinguished lineage: *Publius Claudius Pulcher, son of Publius, grandson of Appius, and great-grandson of Appius. [He was] quaestor, quaesitor, praetor, and augur.* The vase was already 900 years old when it was imported to Rome and bought by Claudius.[30] It is similar to other antique Egyptian pieces selected as final resting places by aristocratic Romans: Claudius was, like his father, a fashionable man. The vase is quite large (nearly two feet tall), and its bright, gleaming stone, set among the sarcophagi in the Claudian family crypt, would have had a striking visual impact on future generations who came to visit.

The only other survivor of Fulvia's brood was her younger son by Antonius, Iullus, who was just a toddler when she died. After Fulvia's death, he continued to live with Octavia. By all accounts, he and his stepmother had a good relationship, and she is credited with arranging his marriage to her daughter, the elder Marcella, after Marcella was divorced from Agrippa, Octavian's powerful general.[31] As a young man, Iullus and his siblings (full, half, and step) enjoyed the best of everything. Octavia's house was a center of lively intellectual conversation,[32] and we know that Iullus studied poetry with L. Crassicius Pansa, who taught the sons of many aristocratic young men of the day and may

---

28. Val. Max. 3.5.3.
29. I follow the reconstruction of the family tree by Wiseman 1970, 220, but see Syme 1986, 148–9. Claudia's trial is reported by Tac., *Ann.* 4.52.
30. *ILS* 882 = *CIL* 6.1282 (from Rome); Swetnam-Burland 2015, 25–8.
31. Plut., *Vit. Ant.* 87.3.
32. Hemelrijk 1999, 104–9.

FIGURE 5.2. Funeral vase of Claudius, son of Fulvia and Clodius.
Source: © Musée du Louvre, Dist. RMN-Grand Palais / Les frères Chuzeville / Art Resource, NY.

have been an old friend of Antonius.[33] Iullus's love of literature extended to creating his own. His poetry receives strong praise from the poet Horace, and a later commentator on Horace reports that Iullus was the author of an epic poem in twelve books on the Greek hero, Diomedes.[34]

Iullus made a good impression on Octavian (now the emperor Augustus), as well. Indeed, Plutarch identifies Iullus, along with Agrippa and Augustus's stepsons, as the people closest to him.[35] Iullus was permitted to engage in politics at the highest levels, serving as praetor in 13 BCE and as consul three years later. Iullus honored his benefactor and emperor with outstanding public entertainments during his praetorship.[36]

---

33. Suet., *Gramm.* 18.1–3. Cicero mentions a Crassicius as one of Antonius's retinue at *Phil.* 13.3. See also Wiseman 1985, who raises the possibility that Crassicius became Augustus's secretary.
34. Pseudo-Acron, commentary on Hor., *Carm.* 4.2.33.
35. Plut., *Vit. Ant.* 87.1.
36. Cass. Dio 54.26.2, with Harders 2009, 233.

His last known assignment was as governor of the province Asia (in what is now Turkey). It is worth noting that Augustus did not trust Iullus with a province that maintained legions.[37] The emperor's good faith had its limits—for good reason, it turns out. Iullus was accused, along with several other aristocratic men, of adultery with Augustus's daughter, Julia, in 2 BCE and, by extension, of desiring to take over as emperor.[38] Iullus committed suicide rather than go through a trial.

Can Fulvia Die?

Such were the lives of the people Fulvia left behind. As for what happened to Fulvia's memory after her death, it is safe to say that more recent centuries have not been any kinder to her than was her own age. In literature, drama, and the visual arts, Fulvia has maintained her reputation as petty, vindictive, and cruel. The story of her abuse of Cicero's disembodied head was a popular motif for European sculptors and painters for centuries.[39] Perhaps the most famous representation is Pavel Svedomsky's *Fulvia with the Head of Cicero* (Figure 5.3).[40] The image is replete with sensuous luxury befitting Rome's most powerful woman: Fulvia is dressed in silks, from under which pokes a foot in a delicate leather slipper. She sits on an animal-skin rug, leaning on a chaise longue that is supported by exquisitely carved legs and is draped in a sky-blue coverlet. An ornate flowerpot sits to the right; it is balanced on the left of the scene by an ornate marble table topped with luscious fruits. Fulvia gazes at Cicero's head with evil delight. She has been playing with it for so long that it has turned a disturbing green color. The viewer can see her hairpins protruding from his tongue and then

---

37. Syme 1986, 144.
38. Vell. Pat. 2.100.4; Plin., *HN* 7.147–9; Sen., *Brev.* 4.6; Cass. Dio 55.10.15. Hallett (2006) argues that Augustus's punishment of Iullus was influenced by the emperor's complex and hostile relationship to Fulvia.
39. For example, sculptures include *Fulvia* by Lio Gangeri (1887), now in the Galleria Nazionale d'Arte Moderna in Rome, and the small ivory figurine *Fulvia mit dem Haupt des Ciceros* from the workshop of Leonhard Kern (first half of seventeenth century), which has been missing from the Badisches Landesmuseum in Karlsruhe, Germany, since at least 2016 (https://www.ka-news.de/region/karlsruhe/Karlsruhe~/Badisches-Landesmuseum-Nicht-nur-Millionen-Diadem-gestohlen;art6066,2078441). Relevant paintings include *Die Rache des Fulvia* (c. 1692) by Gregorio Lazzarini, now in the Staatliche Kunstsammlungen in Kassel, Germany, and Francisco Maura y Montaner's *Fulvia y Marco Antonio, o la venganze de Fulvia* (1888) in the Prado Museum in Madrid, Spain.
40. See Keegan 2020, 119–20.

FIGURE 5.3. P. A. Svedomsky, *Fulvia with the Head of Cicero*, State Open-Air Museum of History and Architecture, Pereslavl Zalessky, Russia.
Source: Album / Alamy Stock Photo).

notices that one remains in Fulvia's hair. Perhaps she has not finished abusing him yet.

In popular literature, Fulvia has generally maintained her ancient role as a supporting player, although sometimes she is erased from history altogether. She was completely written out of one of the most lavish and popular presentations of the Republic in the twenty-first century: the television miniseries *Rome*, a joint production of HBO and the BBC (2005–2007). Even in her own story, she is often reduced to a secondary role. A case in point is Steven Saylor's novelization of Clodius's murder and the ensuing trial, *A Murder on the Appian Way* (2006). Saylor's Fulvia is austere and calculating, even cold. She expresses her grief only in front of a crowd—on the night Clodius's body was displayed to supporters and again in court as the last witness in Milo's trial. Other characters debate whether the grief is genuine. Her main contribution to the plot is to send the novel's protagonist, the fictional detective Gordianus, on a wild goose chase to investigate Antony. Her sister-in-law, Clodia, is a far more fleshed-out character (helpful, seductive, and at times vulnerable) and more essential to the storyline.

The episode of Fulvia's life that most captures the modern literary imagination is how Fulvia must have handled Antony's affair with Cleopatra. But even here, she is not the focus. Emblematic is the treatment she receives in William Shakespeare's *Antony and Cleopatra*, written in 1606–1607, where Fulvia is a driving force of the action. She is a strong presence, even though she never once appears on stage. Right from the beginning, Fulvia looms large in Cleopatra's imagination, on a par with Octavian (Caesar) as twin forces that might take Antony from her. A messenger arrives from Rome; despite her misgivings, Cleopatra urges Antony to hear the news he brings (*Ant.* 1.1.30–37):

You must not stay here longer: your dismission
Is come from Caesar. Therefore hear it, Antony.
Where's Fulvia's process? Caesar's, I would say—
   both?
Call in the messengers. As I am Egypt's queen,
Thou blushest, and that blood of thine
Is Caesar's homager, else so thy cheek pays shame
When shrill-tongued Fulvia scolds. The messengers!

So strong is Fulvia's grip on Cleopatra's imagination that when, a little later (*Ant.* 1.3.70), the queen learns that Fulvia has died, her response is incredulous: *Can Fulvia die?*

Shakespeare's Fulvia is even more warlike than Dio's and Velleius's. Whereas the ancient sources describe only disagreement between Fulvia and Lucius, followed by their unity in opposition to Octavian, the news from Rome in *Antony and Cleopatra* is that Fulvia had first taken up arms against Lucius (*Ant.* 1.1.93–100). Only after that conflict was resolved did a united Antonian party move against Caesar. When they meet face to face in the next act, Caesar blames Antony for not restraining his wife and brother. Antony responds that he did not encourage Lucius and that Caesar would find ruling one-third of the world easier than controlling a woman like Fulvia (*Ant.* 2.2.53–85).

CAESAR: *you may be pleased to catch at mine intent*
By what did here befall me. Your wife and brother
Made wars upon me, and their contestation
Was theme for you: you were the word of war.

ANTONY: *You do mistake your business. My brother never*
Did urge me in his act. I did inquire it,
And have my learning from some true reports
That drew their swords with you. Did he not rather
Discredit my authority with yours,
And make the wars alike against my stomach,

After Fulvia's Death

Having alike your cause? Of this my letters
Before did satisfy you. If you'll patch a quarrel,
As matter whole you have to make it with,
It must not be with this.

CAESAR: *You praise yourself*
By laying defects of judgment to me; but
You patch'd up your excuses.

ANTONY: *Not so, not so.*
I know you could not lack—I am certain on't—
Very necessity of this thought, that I,
Your partner in the cause 'gainst which he fought,
Could not with graceful eyes attend those wars
Which fronted mine own peace. As for my wife,
I would you had her spirit in such another.
The third o' th' world is yours, which with a snaffle
You may pace easy, but not such a wife.

ENOBARBUS: *Would we had all such wives, that the men*
might go to wars with the women!

ANTONY: *So much uncurbable, her garboils, Caesar,*
Made out of her impatience—which not wanted
Shrewdness of policy too—I grieving grant
Did you too much disquiet. For that you must
But say I could not help it.

At least Shakespeare's Antony evinces real respect, if not love, for his wife and her politically savvy "shrewdness of policy." When he first learns of her death (*Ant.* 1.2.137), he credits her: *There's a great spirit gone!*

Fulvia has scarcely fared better in other, more modern recountings of her last act. For example, in Colleen McCullough's *Masters of Rome* series, she is indomitable and calculating from the first moment we see her in *Caesar's Women* (1996). At her initial meeting with her new fiancé, she plants in Clodius's mind the idea of a political career built on catering to the needs to urban populace, and she quickly acquires a reputation for unladylike behavior: "Women didn't frequent the Forum; women didn't listen to comitial meetings from a prominent place;

women didn't raise their voices to shout encouragement and bawdy abuse. Fulvia did all of those...."[41] In the final novel in the series, 2007's *Antony and Cleopatra*, Fulvia is described with adjectives like "warlike" and "termagant," and also as "a good mare"—a reference to her impressive fertility, enhanced by McCullough with an extra two children. This Fulvia is a strong figure who abuses and is abused: Antony reminisces about how Fulvia would take a beating and respond by raking him with her nails. The only time that we see Fulvia herself in this novel is at her final meeting with Antony, in Greece in the aftermath of the failure of Perusia (for which, in this version, she is largely responsible). She greets him as she enters the room, dressed to please him. Antony, in a rage at the embarrassing loss in Italy, turns at the sound of her voice and, before he says anything, lands a blow that knocks her to the floor. The beating that follows knocks out her teeth and breaks her nose. He rages at her for testing Octavian and divorces her on the spot. A few pages later, we learn that Fulvia has committed suicide, so distraught was she over Antony's abandonment—a disappointing and incongruous end for so resourceful and strong-willed a woman.

Fulvia's Legacy

In the late Roman republic, aristocratic Roman women wielded unofficial power behind the scenes but were expected to shrink from drawing too much attention to themselves. Against this backdrop, Fulvia, the daughter of Sempronia and Bambalio, stands out for her fearless political activity and her refusal to be cowed by the private gossip, the public invective, and the open hostility she attracted. The sources, no matter how hostile they might be, show us a woman with real political acuity who was a fierce defender of her husbands' interests and her own, and a valued ally of consuls and generals. It is also important to remember that, behind the hostile rhetoric, is a woman who behaved as a proper *materfamilias*: her husbands succeeded, her children flourished, and her personal reputation almost never admitted even a whiff of sexual scandal—the same cannot be said for her husbands. Perhaps Fulvia's most lasting legacy is that, more than any of her powerful

---

41. McCullough 1996, 386.

contemporaries, she set the mold for the strong imperial women who followed behind her.[42] T. C. Brennan has proposed that Fulvia's handling of Clodius's funeral was in the mind of Agrippina when she brought to Rome the ashes of her recently murdered husband, Germanicus, in 20 CE.[43] Even if such close connections are difficult, if not impossible, to prove, traces of brazen and brash Fulvia, who meddled in men's affairs and who took action when it was necessary, are clear to see in the portrayals of Livia and Agrippina, Plotina, the younger Faustina, and the women of the Severan dynasty. Imperious Fulvia was in many ways the prototype of the imperial woman.

42. Babcock (1965, 32 with earlier references) came to the same conclusion. Fischer identifies Fulvia as the first Roman woman to enter politics in any sort of lasting way (1999, 29).

43. Brennan 2012, 357.

Bibliography

Abbott, F. F. 1909. *Society and Politics in Ancient Rome: Essays and Sketches.* New York: Charles Scribner and Sons.

Alexander, D. A. 2011. "Marc Antony's Assault of Publius Clodius: Fact or Ciceronian Fiction?" in *ASCS 32 Selected Proceedings*, edited by A. Mackay (ascs.org.au/news/ascs32/Alexander.pdf).

Babcock, C. L. 1965. "The Early Career of Fulvia." *American Journal of Philology* 86: 1–32.

Balsdon, J. P. V. D. 1962. *Roman Women, Their History and Habits.* London: Bodley Head.

Barrett, A. A. 2006. "Augustus and the Governor's Wives." *Rheinisches Museum für Philologie* 149: 129–47.

Batstone, W. W., and C. Damon. 2006. *Caesar's Civil War.* Oxford: Oxford University Press.

Bauman, R. A. 1992. *Women and Politics in Ancient Rome.* London: Routledge.

Benedetti, L. 2012. *Glandes Perusinae: Revisione e aggiornamenti.* Opusculua Epigraphica 13. Rome: Quasar.

Borrell, M. 1852. *A Catalogue of the Choice Collection of Greek, Roman, Byzantine and Mediaeval Coins Formed during a Residence of Upwards of Thirty Years in the Levant, by the Late H. P. Borrell, of Smyrna.* London: Davy and Sons.

Bradley, K. 1998. "The Sentimental Education of a Roman Child: The Role of Pet-Keeping." *Latomus* 57: 523–57.

Brennan, T. C. 2012. "Perceptions of Women's Power in the Late Republic: Terentia, Fulvia, and the Generation of 63 BCE," in *A Companion to Women in the Ancient World*, edited by S. L. James and S. Dillon, pp. 354–66. Malden, MA: Wiley-Blackwell.

Brouwer, H. H. J. 1989. *Bona Dea: The Sources and a Description of the Cult.* Leiden: Brill.

Cluett, R. G. 1998. "Roman Women and Triumviral Politics, 43–37 B.C." *Echos du Monde Classique* 42, n.s. 17: 67–84.

Corbett, J. 2003. *West Dickens Avenue: A Marine at Khe Sanh.* New York: Ballantine.

Crawford, J. W. 1994. *M. Tullius Cicero: The Fragmentary Speeches.* 2nd ed. Atlanta, GA: Scholars Press.

Crawford, M. H. 1974. *Roman Republican Coinage.* 2 vols. Cambridge: Cambridge University Press.

Davies, P. J. E. 2017. *Architecture and Politics in Republican Rome*. Cambridge: Cambridge University Press.

De la Bédoyère, G. 2018. *Domina: The Women Who Made Imperial Rome*. New Haven, CT: Yale University Press.

De Souza, P. 1999. *Piracy in the Greco-Roman World*. Cambridge: Cambridge University Press.

Degrassi, A. 1963. *Inscriptiones Italiae 13.2: Fasti Anni Numani et Iuliani*. Rome: Istituto Poligrafico dello Stato.

Delia, D. 1991. "Fulvia Reconsidered," in *Women's History and Ancient History*, edited by S. B. Pomeroy, pp. 197–217. Chapel Hill and London: University of North Carolina Press.

DiLuzio, M. 2016. *A Place at the Altar: Priestesses in Republican Rome*. Princeton, NJ: Princeton University Press.

Dixon, S. 1992. *The Roman Family*. Baltimore, MD: Johns Hopkins University Press.

Epplett, C. 2014. "Roman Beast Hunts," in *A Companion to Sport and Spectacle in Greek and Roman Antiquity*, edited by P. Christesen and D. G. Kyle, pp. 505–19. Chichester, West Sussex, UK: John Wiley and Sons.

Ernout, A., and A. Meillet. 1967. *Dictionnaire étymologique de la langue latine: Histoire des mots*. 4th edition. Paris: Klincksieck.

Evans Grubbs, J. 2005. "Children and Divorce in Roman Law," in *Hoping for Continuity: Childhood, Education and Death in Antiquity and the Middle Ages*, edited by K. Mustakallio, J. Hanska, H.-L. Sainio, and V. Vuolanto, pp. 33–47. Acta Instituti Romani Finlandiae 33. Rome: Institutum Romanum Finlandiae.

Fischer, R. A. 1999. *Fulvia und Octavia: Die beiden Ehefrauen des Marcus Antonius in den politischen Kämpfen der Umbruchszeit zwischen Republik und Principat*. Berlin: Logos.

Gabba, E. 1970. *Appiani Bellorum Civilium Liber Quintus*. Florence: La Nuova Italia Editrice.

Gabba, E. 1971. "The Perusine War and Triumviral Italy." *Harvard Studies in Classical Philology* 75: 139–60.

Gardner, J. F. 1986. *Women in Roman Law and Society*. London: Croom Helm.

Gladhill, B. 2018. "Women from the Rostra: Fulvia and the *Pro Milone*," in *Reading Republican Oratory: Reconstructions, Contexts, Receptions*, edited by C. Gray, A. Balbo, R. M. A. Marshall, and C. E. W. Steel, pp. 297–308. Oxford: Oxford University Press.

Goldsworthy, A. 2010. *Antony and Cleopatra*. New Haven, CT: Yale University Press.

Goldsworthy, A. 2014. *Augustus: The First Emperor of Rome*. New Haven, CT: Yale University Press.

Gowing, A. 1992. *The Triumviral Narratives of Appian and Cassius Dio*. Ann Arbor: University of Michigan Press.

Gray-Fow, M. 2014. "What to Do with Caesarion." *Greece & Rome* 61: 38–67.

Gurval, R. A. 1995. *Actium and Augustus: The Politics and Emotions of War*. Ann Arbor: University of Michigan Press.

Hallett, J. P. 1977. "Perusinae Glandes and the Changing Image of Augustus." *American Journal of Ancient History* 2: 151–71.

Hallett, J. P. 2006. "Fulvia, Mother of Iullus Antonius: New Approaches to the Sources on Julia's Adultery at Rome." *Helios* 33: 149–64.

Hallett, J. P. 2015. "Fulvia: The Representation of an Elite Roman Woman Warrior," in *Women and War in Antiquity*, edited by J. Fabre-Serris and A. Keith, pp. 247–65. Baltimore, MD: Johns Hopkins University Press.

Harders, A.-C. 2009. "An Imperial Family Man: Augustus as Surrogate Father to Marcus Antonius' Children," in *Growing Up Fatherless in Antiquity*, edited by S. R. Hübner and D. M. Ratzan, pp. 217–40. New York: Cambridge University Press.

Harders, A.-C. 2019. "Mark Antony and the Women by His Side," in *Power Couples in Antiquity: Transversal Perspectives*, edited by A. Bielmán Sanchez, pp. 116–35. New York: Routledge.

Head, B. V. 1906. *Catalogue of the Greek Coins of Phrygia*. London: Trustees of the British Museum.

Hemelrijk, E. A. 1999. *Matrona Docta: Educated Women in the Roman Élite from Cornelia to Julia Domna*. London: Routledge.

Hemelrijk, E. A. 2015. *Hidden Lives, Public Personae: Women and Civic Life in the Roman West*. Oxford: Oxford University Press.

Hersch, K. K. 2010. *The Roman Wedding*. New York: Cambridge University Press.

Hoover, O. D. 2012. *Handbook of Coins of Northern and Central Anatolia*. Lancaster: Classical Numismatics Group.

Huzar, E. 1985-6. "Mark Antony: Marriages versus Careers." *Classical Journal* 81: 97–111.

Johnson, C. P. 1972–1973. "Mark Antony, Man of Five Families." *SAN* 4: 21–4.

Kaden, S. 2012. "Verkannte Weiblichkeit? Fulvia in der Erfüllung sozialer Rollen einer Matrona Romana." *Potestas* 5: 83–106.

Kagan, J. 2015. "Maximilian John Borrell (c. 1802–1870): Dealer, Collector, and Forgotten Scholar and the Making of *Historia Numorum*," in ΚΑΙΡΟΣ: *Contributions to Numismatics in Honor of Basil Demetriadi*, edited by U. Wartenberg and M. Amandry, pp. 83–96. New York: American Numismatic Society.

Kaster, R. 1995. *Suetonius: De Grammaticis et Rhetoribus*. Oxford: Clarendon Press.

Kaster, R. 2006. *Marcus Tullius Cicero: Speech on Behalf of Publius Sestius*. Oxford: Clarendon Press.

Keegan, P. 2020. "Colon(ial)izing Fulvia: (Re)presenting the Military Woman in History, Fiction and Art," in *Orientalism and the Reception of Powerful Women in the Ancient World*, edited by F. Carlà-Uhink and A. Wieber, pp. 103–22. London: Bloomsbury.

Keith, A. 2011. "Lycoris Galli/Volumnia Cytheris: A Greek Courtesan in Rome." *EuGeStA* 1: 23–53.

Kelly, G. P. 2006. *A History of Exile in the Roman Republic*. Cambridge: Cambridge University Press.

Keppie, L. 1984. *The Making of the Roman Army*. London: Batsford.

Kleiner, D. E. E. 1992. "Politics and Gender in the Pictorial Propaganda of Antony and Octavian." *Echos du Monde Classique* 36: 357–67.

Konrad, C. F. 1996. "Notes on Roman Also-rans," in *Imperium Sine Fine: T. Robert S. Broughton and the Roman Republic*, edited by J. Linderski, *Historia Einzelschriften* 105, pp. 103–43. Stuttgart: Franz Steiner.

Lacey, W. K. 1961. "The Tribunate of Curio." *Historia* 10: 318–29.

Lange, C. H. 2009. *Res publica constituta: Actium, Apollo and the Accomplishment of the Triumviral Assignment*. Leiden: Brill.

Leach, E. W. 2007. "Claudia Quinta (*Pro Caelio* 34) and an Altar to Magna Mater." *Dictynna* 4 (https://journals.openedition.org/dictynna/157).

Lee, H. M. 2014. "Greek Sports in Rome," in *A Companion to Sport and Spectacle in Greek and Roman Antiquity*, edited by P. Christesen and D. G. Kyle, pp. 533–42. Chichester, West Sussex, UK: John Wiley and Sons.

Levick, B. 2012. "Women and Law," in *A Companion to Women in Antiquity*, edited by S. L. James and S. Dillon, pp. 96–106. Hoboken, NJ: John Wiley and Sons.

Lewis, R. G. 2006. *Asconius: Commentaries on Speeches by Cicero*. Oxford University Press.

Linderski, J. 1972. "The Aedileship of Favonius, Curio the Younger and Cicero's Election to the Augurate." *Harvard Studies in Classical Philology* 76: 181–200.

Linderski, J. 1996. "Q. Scipio Imperator," in *Imperium Sine Fine: T. Robert S. Broughton and the Roman Republic*, edited by J. Linderski, *Historia Einzelschriften* 105, pp. 145–86. Stuttgart: Franz Steiner. Reprinted in J. Linderski, 2007. *Roman Questions II*. HABES 44, pp. 130–74. Stuttgart: Franz Steiner.

Lindsay, H. 2009. *Adoption in the Roman World*. Cambridge: Cambridge University Press.

Lintott, A. 1968. *Violence in Republican Rome*. Oxford: Oxford University Press.

Lintott, A. 1999. *The Constitution of the Roman Republic*. Oxford: Oxford University Press.

Livadiotti, U. 2013. "Lucio Antonio, Appiano e la propaganda augustea." *Seminari romani di cultura greca* 2: 81–5.

Logghe, L. 2016. "The Gentleman Was Not for Turning: The Alleged *volte-face* of Gaius Scribonius Curio." *Latomus* 75: 353–77.

Manuwald, G. 2007. *Cicero, Philippics 3–9*. 2 vols. Berlin: De Gruyter.

Manuwald, G. 2011. *Roman Republican Theatre*. Cambridge: Cambridge University Press.

Marshall, B. A. 1985. *A Historical Commentary on Asconius*. Columbia: University of Missouri Press.

Mattingly, H. 1960. *Roman Coins from the Earliest Times to the Fall of the Western Empire*. 2nd edition. Chicago: Quadrangle Books.

McCracken, G. 1942. "The Villa and the Tomb of Lucullus at Tusculum." *American Journal of Archaeology* 46: 325–40.

McCullough, C. 1996. *Caesar's Women*. New York: William Morrow.

McDermott, W. C. 1972. "Curio Pater and Cicero." *American Journal of Philology* 93: 381–411.

Morrell, K. 2015. "Cato, Caesar, and the Germani." *Antichthon* 49: 73–93.

Morstein-Marx, R. 2007. "Caesar's Alleged Fear of Prosecution and His *Ratio Absentis* in the Approach to the Civil War." *Historia* 56: 159–78.

Morstein-Marx, R. 2009. "*Dignitas* and *res publica*: Caesar and Republican Legitimacy," in *Eine politische Kultur (in) der Krise? Die "letzte Generation" der roemischen Republik*, edited by K.-J. Hölkeskamp, pp. 115–40. Munich: De Gruyter.

Münzer, F. 1999. *Roman Aristocratic Parties and Families*. Translated by T. Ridley. Baltimore, MD: Johns Hopkins University Press.

Naspi, A., and E. Radaelli. 2011. "S(hort) M(essage) S(ervice) *ante litteram*: Antichi proiettili iscritti ed insulti di guerra." *Forma Urbis* 16: 4–7.

Nisbet, R. G. 1939. *M. Tulli Ciceronis De Domo Sua Ad Pontifices Oratio*. Oxford: Clarendon Press.

Olson, K. 2008. *Dress and the Roman Woman*. New York: Routledge.

Osgood, J. 2006a. *Caesar's Legacy: Civil War and the Emergence of the Roman Empire*. Cambridge: Cambridge University Press.

Osgood, J. 2006b. "Eloquence under the Triumvirs." *American Journal of Philology* 127: 525–51.

Osgood, J. 2014. *Turia: A Roman Woman's Civil War*. New York: Oxford University Press.

Pelling, C. B. R. 1988. *Plutarch: Life of Antony*. Cambridge: Cambridge University Press.

Ramsey, J. T. 2003. *Philippics I–II*. Cambridge: Cambridge University Press.

Ramsey, J. T. 2004. "Did Julius Caesar Temporarily Banish Mark Antony from His Inner Circle?" *Classical Quarterly* 54: 161–73.

Ramsey, J. T. 2009. "The Proconsular Years: Politics at a Distance," in *A Companion to Caesar*, edited by M. Griffin, pp. 37–56. Malden, MA: Blackwell.

Rawson, B. 2003. *Children and Childhood in Roman Italy*. Oxford: Oxford University Press.

Ridley, R. T. 1999. "What's in a Name: The So-Called First Triumvirate." *Arctos* 33: 133–44.

Riggsby, A. M. 2002. "Clodius/Claudius." *Historia* 51: 117–23.

Rihil, T. 2009. "Lead 'Slingshot' (*Glandes*)." *Journal of Roman Archaeology* 22: 146–69.

Rizzelli, G. 2006. "Antonio e Fadia." *Rudiae* 18: 201–20.

Roddaz, J.-M. 1988. "Lucius Antonius." *Historia* 37: 317–46.

Roller, D. W. 2003. *The World of Juba II and Kleopatra Selene: Royal Scholarship on Rome's African Frontier*. New York: Routledge.

Roller, D. W. 2010. *Cleopatra: A Biography*. New York: Oxford University Press.

Roller, D. W. 2018. *Cleopatra's Daughter and Other Royal Women of the Augustan Era*. New York: Oxford University Press.

Rosillo López, C. 2013. "The Common (*Mediocris*) Orator of the Late Republic: The Scribonii Curiones," in *Community and Communication: Oratory and Politics in Republican Rome*, edited by C. Steel and H. van der Blom, pp. 287–98. Oxford: Oxford University Press.

Rüpke, J. 2011. *The Roman Calendar from Numa to Constantine: Time, History, and the Fasti*. Translated by D. M. B. Richardson. Malden, MA: Wiley-Blackwell.

Russell, A. 2016. *The Politics of Public Space in Republican Rome*. Cambridge: Cambridge University Press.

Sanders, H. A. 1932. "The So-Called First Triumvirate." *MAAR* 10: 55–68.

Schultze, C. 2007. "Making a Spectacle of Oneself: Pliny on Curio's Theatre," in *Vita Vigilia Est: Essays in Honour of Barbara Levick*, edited by E. Bispham and G. Rowe, pp. 127–45. London: Institute of Classical Studies.

Seager, R. 2002. *Pompey the Great: A Political Biography*. 2nd edition. Malden, MA: Blackwell.

Sear, F. 2006. *Roman Theatres: An Architectural Study*. Oxford: Oxford University Press.

Shackleton Bailey, D. R. 1977. "Brothers or Cousins?" *American Journal of Ancient History* 2: 148–9.

Shackleton Bailey, D. R. 1991. *Cicero, Back from Exile: Six Speeches upon His Return*. Chicago: American Philological Association.

Sims-Williams, P. 2013. "The Celtic Composition Vowels -o- and -io-," in *Continental Celtic Word Formation: The Onomastic Data*, edited by J. L. García Alonso, pp. 37–50. Salamanca: Universidad de Salamanca.

Skinner, M. B. 2011. *Clodia Metelli: The Tribune's Sister*. Oxford and New York: Oxford University Press.

Šterbenc Erker, D. 2011. "Gender and Roman Funeral Ritual," in *Memory and Mourning: Studies on Roman Death*, edited by V. M. Hope and J. Huskinson, pp. 40–60. Oxford: Oxbow Books.

Sumi, G. S. 1997. "Power and Ritual: The Crowd at Clodius' Funeral." *Historia* 46: 80–102.

Swetnam-Burland, M. 2015. *Egypt in Italy: Visions in Egypt in Roman Imperial Culture*. New York: Cambridge University Press.

Syme, R. 1964. *Sallust*. Berkeley: University of California Press.

Syme, R. 1986. *The Augustan Aristocracy*. Oxford: Clarendon Press.

Syme, R. 2016. *Approaching the Roman Revolution: Papers on Republican History*. Edited by F. Santangelo. Oxford: Oxford University Press.

Tatum, W. J. 1991. "Cicero, the Elder Curio, and the Titinia Case." *Mnemosyne* 44: 364–71.

Tatum, W. J. 1992. "The Poverty of the Claudii Pulchri: Varro, De Re Rustica 3.16.1–2." *Classical Quarterly* 42: 190–200.

Tatum, W. J. 1999. *The Patrician Tribune*. Chapel Hill: University of North Carolina Press.

Taylor, L. R. 1942. "Caesar's Colleagues in the Pontifical College." *American Journal of Philology* 63: 385–412.

Toher, M. 2004. "Octavian's Arrival in Rome, 44 B.C." *Classical Quarterly* 54: 174–84.

Traina, G. 2001. "Lycoris the Mime," in *Roman Women*, edited by A. Fraschetti, translated by L. Lapin, pp. 82–99. Chicago: University of Chicago Press.

Treggiari, S. 1991. *Roman Marriage: Iusti Coniuges from the Time of Cicero to the Time of Ulpian*. Oxford: Clarendon Press.

Treggiari, S. 2007. *Terentia, Tullia and Publilia: The Women of Cicero's Family.* London: Routledge.

Treggiari, S. 2019. *Servilia and Her Family.* Oxford: Oxford University Press.

Virlouvet, C. 2001. "Fulvia the Woman of Passion," in *Roman Women*, edited by A. Fraschetti, translated by L. Lapin, pp. 66–81. Chicago: University of Chicago Press.

Waddington, W. H. 1853. *Voyage en Asie-Mineure au point de vue numismatique.* Paris: La Revue Numismatique.

Weir, A. J. 2007. "A Study of Fulvia." Master's thesis, Queen's University.

Welch, K. E. 1995. "Antony, Fulvia, and the Ghost of Clodius in 47 B.C." *Greece & Rome* 42: 182–201.

Welch, K. E. 2012. *Magnus Pius.* Swansea: Classical Press of Wales.

Welch, K. E. forthcoming. "Memorable Women and Women in the Memory of Civil War," in *A Culture of Civil War*, edited by W. Havener. HABES. Stuttgart: Franz Steiner.

Wirszubski, Ch. 1961. "*Audaces*: A Study in Political Phraseology." *Journal of Roman Studies* 51: 12–22.

Wiseman, T. P. 1968. "Two Friends of Clodius in Cicero's Letters." *Classical Quarterly* 18: 297–302.

Wiseman, T. P. 1970. "Pulcher Claudius." *Harvard Studies in Classical Philology* 74: 207–21. Reprinted in Wiseman, *Roman Studies, Literary and Historical*, pp. 42–56. Liverpool: Francis Cairns, 1987.

Wiseman, T. P. 1985. "Who Was Crassicius Pansa?" *Transactions of the American Philological Association* 115: 187–96. Reprinted in Wiseman, *Historiography and Imagination: Eight Essays on Roman Culture*, pp. 90–7. Exeter: University of Exeter Press, 1994.

Wood, S. E. 1999. *Imperial Women: A Study in Public Images, 40 B.C.-A. D. 68.* Leiden: Brill.

Ypsilanti, M. 2018. *The Epigrams of Crinagoras of Mytilene.* Oxford: Oxford University Press.

Zangemeister, C. 1885. *Glandes Plumbeae Latinae Inscriptae*, in the series *Ephemeris Epigraphica* 6. Rome: Institutum Archaeologicum Romanum.

Index

For the benefit of digital users, indexed terms that span two pages (e.g., 52–53) may, on occasion, appear on only one of those pages.

Figures are indicated by *f* following the page number

actors, 11–12, 44–45, 65, 66, 83–84
Aemilius Lepidus, M., triumvir, 60, 73, 75–76, 79–81, 86–87, 88, 89–90, 91, 92–94, 96, 100–1, 104, 105
Agrippa. *See* Vipsanius Agrippa
Alexander Helios, son of Antonius and Cleopatra, 64*f*, 105–6, 108
Annius Milo, T., tribune of 57 BCE, 40–48, 52, 54, 66–67, 114
Antonia, first wife of Antonius, 64*f*, 67, 81–82, 85
Antonia, daughter of Antonius and Antonia, 64*f*, 67, 68, 86–87, 105–6, 110
Antonia Maior, daughter of Antonius and Octavia, 64*f*, 105–6, 109–10
Antonia Minor, daughter of Antonius and Octavia, 64*f*, 105–6, 109–10
Antonius, C., praetor of 44 BCE, 66–67, 76, 78, 79
Antonius, Iullus, 9*f*, 64*f*, 68, 94, 105–6, 110, 111–13
Antonius, L., consul 41 BCE, 7n.9, 64*f*, 66–67, 76, 92–103, 104, 115
Antonius, M., triumvir, 1, 2, 3, 5–6, 7, 9*f*, 14–16, 29–30, 35, 37, 45–46, 51, 52–54, 59, 60, 61–72, 64*f*, 73–103, 104–8, 109–12, 114–17
Antonius Antyllus, M., 9*f*, 64*f*, 68, 75–76, 82–84, 94, 105–6, 108, 110

Antonius Hybrida, C., consul of 63, 12–13, 62–63, 64*f*
Antony. *See* M. Antonius
Antyllus, M. Antonius Antyllus
Atticus. *See* T. Pomponius Atticus
Augustus. *See* C. Julius Caesar (Octavian)
Aurelia, mother of Julius Caesar, 32–34

Bona Dea, 32–35, 37–39, 40, 42–43, 51, 52
Brutus. *See* M. Junius Brutus

Caecilius Metellus Celer, Q., consul of 60 BCE, 21*f*, 22–23, 29–30, 37–38
Caelius Rufus, M., lover of Clodia Metelli, 22–23, 45–46, 49–50, 52–53, 58, 66–67, 84–85
Caesarion. *See* Ptolemy XV Caesarion
Cassius Longinus, C., assassin of Caesar, 72, 75–77, 78–79, 86–87, 88, 91–92, 93–94, 104
Catiline. *See* L. Sergius Catilina
Cato. *See* M. Porcius Cato
Catullus. *See* C. Valerius Catullus
Cicero. *See* M. Tullius Cicero
Claudia, daughter of Fulvia and Clodius, 9*f*, 21*f*, 36–37, 59–60, 68, 86–87, 89–90, 94, 104, 110–11
Claudia, Vestal Virgin, 23–24, 25*f*
Claudia Quinta, 23–24, 24*f*

Claudius Caecus (the Blind), Ap., censor of 312 BCE, 20, 41–42, 84–85
Claudius Pulcher, Ap., consul of 79 BCE, 21f, 25, 32–33, 111
Claudius Pulcher, Ap., consul of 54 BCE, 21f, 25–28, 33, 39, 44, 53–55
Claudius Pulcher, C., praetor of 56 BCE, 21f, 26–27, 33, 44, 54–55
Claudius Pulcher, P., consul of 249 BCE, 20–22
Claudius Pulcher, P. son of Fulvia and Clodius, praetor after 31 BCE, 9f, 21f, 36–37, 46, 59–60, 68, 110–11, 112f
Cleopatra VII, queen of Egypt, 4–5, 16, 29–30, 61, 64f, 73–74, 91–92, 95–96, 103, 105–8, 110, 114–17
Cleopatra Selene, daughter of Antonius and Cleopatra, 64f, 105–7, 108–9, 110
Clodia Metelli, sister-in-law of Fulvia, 21f, 22–23, 29–30, 37–38, 45–46, 49–50, 52–53, 65, 84–86, 114
Clodius Pulcher, P., tribune of the plebs 58 BCE, 3, 4, 5, 6–8, 9f, 18, 19–48, 49–55, 58, 66–67, 82, 85–86, 111, 114, 116–18
Cornelius Dolabella, P., consul of 44 BCE, 59–60, 66–67, 76, 79
Cornelius Sulla, L., dictator 82–?80, 5–6, 31–32, 50–51, 60, 87–89
Crassus. *See* M. Licinius Crassus
Curio. *See* C. Scribonius Curio
Cytheris. *See* Volumnia Cytheris

Dolabella. *See* P. Cornelius Dolabella

equestrians, 5–6, 7–8, 51, 63–65, 96, 100–1

Fadia, 63, 64f, 66–67, 81–82, 83, 84–85
Fulvia, member of Catilinarian conpiracy, 12–13
Fulvia, daughter of Sempronia and Bambalio, *passim*
 abuse of Cicero's corpse, 4, 88–89, 113–14, 114f
 childhood, 8–18, 83–84
 children, 19–20, 36–37, 41, 46, 48, 50–51, 59–60, 68, 74–75, 94, 100–1, 102, 110–13

 coins, 14–16, 14f
 death, 5, 103, 116–17
 family, 1, 8–13, 9f, 83–85
 marriages, 4–5, 18, 19, 34–37, 39–40, 51, 53–57, 67–69, 85–86, 117–18
 physical appearance, 13–16, 14f
 political opinions, 7, 10, 95
 positive assessment of, 4–5, 96
 profited from the Proscriptions, 87–89
 role in aftermath of Clodius' death, 1, 4, 43–45, 46–47, 48, 74, 114, 117–18
 sources hostile toward, 3–4, 73–74, 83, 92–93, 101 (*see also* invective)
 war at Perusia, 74, 92–103, 115–17
Fulvius Flaccus, M., consul of 125 BCE, 10–11
Fulvius Bambalio, M., father of Fulvia, 1, 8–10, 9f, 11, 12, 16–17, 18, 24–25, 35–36, 83–85, 117–18
funerals and funeral games, 43–45, 46–47, 54–57, 117–18

gladiators, 39, 42–43, 55–56, 74–75
Glaphyra, 91–92, 95–96, 100
Gracchus. *See* Sempronius Gracchus

Hortensia, 90

invective, 2, 4–5, 22–23, 29–30, 49–50, 51, 65, 66–67, 68, 73–74, 80, 81–82, 83–86, 88, 90, 98–100, 101, 106

Julia, daughter of Octavian and Scribonia, 106, 112–13
Julia, sister of Julius Caesar, 32, 33–34, 64f
Julia, mother of Antonius, 62–63, 64f, 80, 81–83, 85, 88, 89–90, 100, 101, 102–3, 104
Julius Caesar, C., dictator, 3–4, 7–8, 26–27, 29–30, 31, 32–35, 37–39, 40–41, 50–51, 52–53, 55–56, 57–66, 64f, 67, 68–72, 73–80, 83–84, 86, 101–2, 106, 108
Julius Caesar, C. (Octavian), future emperor Augustus, 1, 3–6, 9f, 16, 73, 74, 77–103, 104–17
Junius Brutus, Dec., assassin of Caesar, 76, 78, 79, 80–81, 82–83, 86–87

128 Index

Junius Brutus, M., assassin of Caesar, 65–66, 72, 75–77, 78–79, 81, 83, 86–87, 88, 91–92, 93–94, 101, 104

Lepidus. *See* >M. Aemilius Lepidus
Lesbia. *See* Clodia Metelli
Libertas, shrine of, 39–40, 48
Liberty. *See* Libertas
Licinius Crassus, M., consul of 55, 7–8, 12, 31, 37–38, 39, 40–41, 49, 52, 71
Licinius Lucullus, L., consul of 74 BCE, 8–10, 21f, 26, 27–28, 30–31
Licinius Murena, L., consul of 62 BCE, 12, 18, 30–32, 33–34, 35–36
Lucullus. *See* L. Licinius Lucullus

Manius, 92, 95–96, 100, 102–3
Marcius Rex, Q., consul of 68 BCE, 21f, 28
Milo. *See* T. Annius Milo
Munatius Plancus, L., consul of 42, 91, 96–97, 102
Murena. *See* L. Licinius Murena

Natta. *See* L. Pinarius Natta
nomenclature, 11, 37–38, 45–46n.73, 65–66, 68, 77

Octavia, third wife of Antonius, 9f, 16, 64f, 89–90, 101, 105–7, 108, 109–10, 111–12
Octavian. *See* C. Julius Caesar (Octavian)
Octavius, C.. *See* C. Julius Caesar (Octavian)
optimates, 7–8, 40–41

Patrician, 6, 7, 20, 37–38
Pinarius Natta, L., pontifex, 9f, 12, 17, 40, 48
pirates, 5, 28, 49–50, 62–63, 69
Plancus. *See* L. Munatius Plancus
plebeians, 6, 7, 37–38, 52
Pompeia, wife of Caesar, 32–34
Pompeius Magnus, Cn., consul of 70, 55, and 52, 7–8, 26–28, 30, 31–32, 37–38, 39, 40–41, 42, 44–48, 49, 52–53, 54, 55–56, 58–61, 66, 68–69, 71–72, 74–75, 79–80, 82, 108

Pompeius, Sextus, son of Pompeius Magnus, 79–81, 86–87, 88, 91, 93, 101–3, 104, 105, 106
Pompey. *See* Pompeius
Pomponius Atticus, T., 29–30, 32–33, 52–53, 63–65, 77, 78–80, 83, 86
pontifex, 12, 39–40
populists, 7–8, 10
Porcia, 91, 101
Porcius Cato, M., 45–46, 58, 60, 101
Ptolemy XIII, brother and husband of Cleopatra VII, 61
Ptolemy XV Caesarion, son of Cleopatra and Caesar, 3n.6, 61, 64f, 108, 110
Ptolemy XVI Philadelphus, son of Cleopatra and Antonius, 64f, 106–7, 108

Scribonius Curio, C., cos. 76 BCE, 29–30, 49, 51, 52–53, 54–56
Scribonius Curio, C. tribune of the plebs 50 BCE, 7, 9f, 29–30, 49, 50–61, 66–67, 85–86, 108
Scribonius Curio, C., son of Fulvia and Curio, 9f, 51, 59–60, 68, 105–6, 108, 110
Sempronia, member of the Catilinarian conspiracy, 12–13, 17–18, 34–35
Sempronia, mother of Fulvia, 1, 9f, 10, 11–13, 16–17, 18, 32, 34, 35, 39–40, 47, 117–18
Sempronius Gracchus, C. tribune of the plebs 123-1 BCE, 10
Sempronius Gracchus, T., tribune of the plebs 133 BCE, 10
Sempronius Tuditanus, C., consul of 129, 9f, 10, 11–12, 24–25
Sempronius Tuditanus, son of consul of 129, 9f, 11–12, 83–84
Sergius Catilina, L., conspirator, 12–13, 29, 31–32, 34–35, 38–39, 62–63
Servilia, 91, 101
Shakespeare, W. 107, 114–16
sling bullets, 97–100
Sulla. *See* L. Cornelius Sulla

Index 129

Terentia, wife of Cicero, 59–60, 66, 82, 100
Tullia, daughter of Cicero, 30, 49, 59–60, 66–67
Tullius Cicero, M., consul 63 BCE, 1, 3, 4–5, 8–10, 11, 12–13, 20, 22–25, 26–27, 29–30, 31, 32–34, 35, 38–41, 42–43, 45–46, 47–48, 49–54, 58, 59–60, 62–68, 69, 70–71, 74, 75–76, 77–87, 88–89, 100, 101, 110–11, 113–14

Tullius Cicero, Q., praetor of 62 BCE, 39, 59

Valerius Catullus, C., poet, 22–23, 30
Vestal Virgins, 23–24, 25f, 30–31, 32–33, 40, 47
Vipsanius Agrippa, M., 96–97, 111–13
Volumnia Cytheris, 63–67, 64f, 68, 80, 81–82, 83–86, 95–96
Volumnius Eutrapelus, P., 63–66, 83